SACRAMENTO

VOLVOX:

Poetry from the Unofficial Languages of Canada
... in English Translation

VOLVOX:

Poetry from the Unofficial Languages of Canada . . . in English Translation

Editor J. MICHAEL YATES
Associate Editor CHARLES LILLARD
Managing Editor ANN J. WEST

1971

The Sono Nis Press P.O. BOX 94, PORT CLEMENTS
THE QUEEN CHARLOTTE ISLANDS, BRITISH COLUMBIA

Copyright © 1971
by The Sono Nis Press

Publication of this anthology
was made possible through assistance
from The Canada Council

Designed and printed by
MORRISS PRINTING COMPANY LTD.
VICTORIA, BRITISH COLUMBIA, CANADA

ACKNOWLEDGEMENTS

GEORGE FALUDY. *Ave Luna, Morituri Te Salutant* first appeared in THE TAMARACK REVIEW and has been broadcast by C.B.C.'s *Anthology.*

HENDRIKAS NAGYS. *Fragments of Childhood* first appeared in LITHUANUS; *Journey into the Night* in DECEMBER; *Oaks* in THE HUDSON REVIEW. In the original Lithuanian: *Medziai* (*Wind in the Trees*) is from LAPKRICIO NAKTYS (Freiburg, 1947). *Pastorale* (*Pastoral*), *Apokalipse* (*Apocalypse*), *Terra Incognito* and *Kelione Naktin* (*Journey into the Night*) are from MELYNAS SNIEGAS (Boston, 1960).

TULIN ERBAS. *As Tender Gifts, Women in Paradise, Go to Sleep, Mermaids, July if You Like,* and *Keep a Khayyam Beauty* first appeared in the Turkish magazine, HISAR.

NICHOLAS CATANOY. *Textes No. 1, Textes No. 6, Clepsydra, Winter Instant,* and *Aegri Somnia* appeared in FLUX ALB (Rumanian and French poems, 1970).

BOGDAN CZAYKOWSKI. *Ars Poetica, Evening Scene,* and *Hourglass* first appeared in English in EXPRESSION; *The Garden* in CONTEMPORARY LITERATURE IN TRANSLATION. *Age de la Pierre I* in EXPLORATIONS IN FREEDOM (New York, The Free Press, 1970). *The Garden, Ars Poetica, Evening Scene,* and *Hourglass* were published in CONTEMPORARY POETRY OF BRITISH COLUMBIA (Vancouver, The Sono Nis Press, 1970). Polish: *Evening Scene* is from TRZCINY CZCIONEK (London, 1957); *The Collective, Age de la Pierre I & II, The Garden,* and *Ars Poetica* from SPOR Z GRANICAMI (Paris, 1964); *The Explication of Sura* from SURA (London, 1961).

WALTER BAUER. *Leaving the Apartment, Emigrants, From Seven at Night till Four in the Morning, This is the Hour for the Drunk to Sleep, A Midwife Speaks, The Paper-boy,* and *This is not the Way Men Screamed* appeared in THE PRICE OF MORNING in Henry Beissel's translation (Vancouver, Prism International Press, 1968).

GUTTORMUR J. GUTTORMSSON. *These bones were Wages* first appeared in Icelandic in HUNANGSFLUGUR.

SAMAR ATTAR. *The Seer* will be included in a forthcoming anthology edited by Gwendolyn MacEwen.

MANUEL BETANZOS-SANTOS. Selections included here are from CANCION DEL NINO EN LA VENTANA (New York, 1970).

RACHEL H. KORN. *The Housemaid* first appeared in English on C.B.C.'s *Anthology.*

ROBERT ZEND. The selections included here are from FROM ZERO TO ONE translated by John Robert Colombo.

REINHARD WALZ. The selections in this volume have appeared previously in English in CONTEMPORARY LITERATURE IN TRANSLATION.

ANDRZEJ BUSZA. The poems included here have appeared in various periodicals in English: CONTEMPORARY LITERATURE IN TRANSLATION, EXPRESSION, MUNDUS ARTIUM, and PRISM INTERNATIONAL. All have been included in the English-language collection, ASTROLOGER IN THE UNDERGROUND (Athens, Ohio University Press, 1971).

STEPHAN G. STEPHANSSON. The two poems which appear here are from ANDVOKUR.

ROBERT BRUNNER. *The Evening* and *It's an Inexorable Irony* have appeared previously in Russian in the Russian-Language magazine, LA RENAISSANCE.

J. I. SEGAL. Some of the poems here have appeared in English previously in Miss Waddington's translation on C.B.C.'s *Anthology*.

HANNES OJA. *Stones* and *Thought* were published in his Estonian collection, MARGID MOTTELIIVAL (Stockholm, 1964).

LUIGI ROMEO. *Penetanguishene in October* has appeared previously in VITA LATINA.

ANDREAS SCHROEDER. *The Edge* has been published previously in English by MUNDUS ARTIUM.

WACLAW IWANIUK. *Epilogue* and *All that is mine* first appeared in English in BOOKS ABROAD. *Who Calls What a Poem* first appeared in English in EXPLORATIONS IN FREEDOM (New York, The Free Press, 1970).

EINAR PALL JONSSON. *The Laundress* first appeared in his Icelandic collection, SOLHEIMAR.

PAVEL JAVOR. *The Autumn* first appeared in RECOLTE PAUVRE (Paris, Edition Rencontres, 1965). *Far From You* in THE UNIVERSITY OF TORONTO QUARTERLY and RECOLTE PAUVRE. *Silence Falls* in PEN IN EXILE (London, 1960). *All of You* in DELTA MAGAZINE. *The Torpor* in RECOLTE PAUVRE. *The Exile* in PEN IN EXILE.

RAMON MANSOOR. *Yesterday* and *Remember* were published in the Ottawa Spanish-language literary review, REFLEXION. They have also appeared in Spanish in the author's collection, LIRIO ENAMORADO (Castile, 1969).

YAR SLAVUTYCH. *Your Eyes* first appeared in OAZA (Edmonton, 1960). *The House* in TROFEJI (Edmonton, 1963); and an English version was published in CANADIAN LITERATURE. *Epilogue* in ROZSTRILIANA MUZA (Detroit, 1955). *The Days are Short* in SPRAHA (Frankfurt, 1950); in English it appeared in OASIS, SELECTED POEMS BY YAR SLAVUTYCH (New York, 1959).

The Editors wish to express special thanks to

John Robert Colombo
John Reeves
Haraldur Bessasson
Julie Ridley
and Ann J. West

for their aid in gathering this anthology into manuscript form

CONTENTS

If a poet would work politically, he must give himself up to a party; and so soon as he does that he is lost as a poet; he must bid farewell to his free spirit, his unbiased view, and draw over his ears the cap of bigotry and blind hatred.

The poet, as man and citizen, will love his native land; but the native land of his poetic powers and poetic action . . . is confined to no particular province or country . . . . Therein he is like the eagle, who hovers with free gaze over whole countries, and to whom it is of no consequence whether the hare on which he pounces is running in Prussia or in Saxony.

— GOETHE

T. HIRAMATUS

THE FISH

A long way from home
They have been brought
And yet, these goldfish . . .
Already seem to enjoy
Swimming in Canadian Waters.

Translated from the Japanese
by Robert Y. Kadoguchi

GEORGE FALUDY

AVE LUNA, MORITURI TE SALUTANT

1 *In praise of the moon*

Mere moon, I would not notice you,
I'd only bay at you, mere light,
but you are coloured green and smell of lilacs
and you are coloured amber, fat and bloated,
and translucid and bloodshot
and you are more than mere moon,
not just a light, a signal
not just a sign, a symbol
not just a view, a vista,
a disk at dusk, a discus,
companion on my brief
journey to nowhere, like the trees,
mists, grasses, fingernails.

I nearly touched you as a child
with my hands, fetish of mystery,
a bright coin carelessly dropped
you rolled under the skirts of clouds,
you sprinkled flour on Grandfather's mill
the cemetery and the cows
a distant millstone in the sky.

Full moon, my young years' semaphore,
I celebrated you with the firewheels
of sound, simile and metaphor,
Ophelia's mad breast floating naked
in the dark waters of the sky,
a clock-face cut of marble
in hopeless love with untouchable time
dropping its useless hands,

a transcendental angel's rump
sitting tranquil
on heaven's latrine
Hercules' adolescent scrotum
as his mother applies the powder-puff
before his virgin rendezvous.

Giant spider, you caught for me in your web
Cornwall, the Ile-de-France, the hills
of Transylvania and Tuscany,
on seashores, meadows, balconies and rooftops,
in parks and boats, upon the copper-plated
battlements of Amar's
tower in the desert of Morocco
over the crowded camel-humps
of sand dunes:
you played your game of chess against my naked
lovers' bodies — I only watched you play —
and if you bent too close their open thighs
they butted you aside, for I had taught them
to play with you, silver balloon of love.

Aboard battleships, at Saipan, Tarawa,
you'd always aim a merciless
searchlight straight in my eye: I'd run or stand
in total darkness next to black trickles
of springs shot dead and fountains still alive
my chest
bedecked with your medals of mercury;
and how you shone after the war
over Fifth Avenue and Budapest
round, well-fed silver carp
I watched you floating
sprinkling your roe along the Milky Way
and I began to hope,
under your sign the beerhall of the sky

still welcomed guests of every constellation
each in his favourite place
to regularly meet night after night
though many chairs stood empty at my table.

Seven times seven bars, double barbed wire,
and two more lines of barbed wire beyond
the window of the punishment cell at Recsk.
Past the wire only the bluefox firtrees,
shadows of death —
I stepped into the rigid tinfoil
of your cold rays and quietly thought
a transmission belt
a Jacob's ladder
parallel rails running with me
to the white terminal
of eternity —
but Stalin died and left me all alone.

I wouldn't mind seeing you still today
the same as forty years ago
climbing up slowly, red-beard dwarf,
along some gnarled trunks of oaks,
or make you once again a tangerine,
balloon, ideal cheese, shaving mirror
that absconded with a foamy face,
but I shall not complain —
you did follow me faithfully
to Vienna, London, Malta
and once more across the sea
while staying fairly put at home;
only last November in New Jersey
at Andy Hamza's house
full of music, books and symposia
stepping outside the glass doors
I drew quick breaths of pleasure seeing you

on the asphalt-hued branches of the sky:
silver apple in my winter garden,
frozen apple in my winter garden.

By that time I knew that they would reach you
or rather that they would reach your namesake
the satellite, the planet circling
around us, three hundred eighty-four thousand
kilometers away, the objective moon
which, as other bodies, contains its functions
and occupies a space in space
and equals only its own self, the moon
that's only so much and no more, no legend,
anxiety, toy, magic or hypnosis,
godhead, memory and all your other faces,
the real moon, that revolves in distant skies,
of which I'm no part as I am of yours
who are in me and would not exist outside —
so they will reach the moon,
I thought, and I was glad
that they would reach it in my lifetime
and I could keep you still for comfort
and sacrament under the black
cupola of the night and of my old age
and even in the brutal crypt of space
for my death candle.

2 *The conquest of the moon*

Eureka, shouted Archimedes
in the bathtub and a single jump
took him into the streets of Syracuse
to proclaim from the rooftops the news
that the apparent loss in weight etcetera;
"Land, land!" yelled the lookout

from the masthead at two in the morning:
Mary, mother of God, he was right after all,
the captain, this loud-mouthed, greasy faced,
slavedriving fake-Italian
sham-Christian kike;
he will not have to walk the plank at dawn,
we've reached the treasured shores of India!
And only sixty years ago a crease
in the clouds: Wilbur Wright entering Paris!
Along the Bois, in gardens, parks,
a biplane on every strip of grass,
dressed in straw hats and checkered pants
eternal adolescents would
tinker at night: I can still
smell their carbide-lamps and the blood,
airframes made of rulers, walking-sticks,
bedspreads lifted from hotels
or their aunts' old skirts the wings,
and how did their engines spit and sneeze
and what savage cries would rise
to heaven, when one of their grotesque
grasshoppers cleared a bush or two!
Then came the trees, later the hills,
the Channel, the Alps, the sea, the ocean.

"Moon, moon!" I thought before the picture tube
waiting for the great act
(no small time stuff, Columbus, Bleriot)
listening to a commentator who
was demonstrating on a full-scale model
how when and where would Armstrong and Aldrin
emerge from the module and how many yards
would they walk after having cleared the ladder
take photographs put lunar soil in sacks
exchange a few words with president Nixon

raise a flag after the lapse of a certain time
by what process would they re-enter the spacecraft
how many pounds of ballast would they leave
behind how many seismographs — and as the broadcast
was not on schedule, he began to talk
about early utopias of space
mixing Aristarchos up with Lucianos, Samos
with Samosata, pronouncing Cyrano
as Kyrano, and telling us finally
that we may celebrate
for in this historic moment
mankind has entered the lunar age.

He repeated all this three more times
when the desert-like moonscape
appeared in a black sky
with the Eagle's contours like an old stove
standing in a museum of science,
then the transparent phantom
of Armstrong's abdomen, then Aldrin
as they tip-toed, then walked and photographed
according to plan, faultless and precise
performing as predicted, as if a bizarre
exercise in gymnastics
wearing barbarous masks, while the younger
generation grew restless watching the screen,
lit cigarettes, giggled: these two
have been shuffling their feet for half an hour
and still there's nothing, not a single shot
has been fired, a dragging production,
so it's been done, we've seen it, is that all?
Man lands on moon is technology triumphant,
boredom supreme.

But I stayed on with the older
people in front of the set: kept yawning,

and hoping that perhaps this once
after Hitler and Stalin
after Rotterdam, Belgrade, Oradour, Coventry,
Katyn Auschwitz, Warsaw, Dresden
after Nikita Kruschev, Lyndon Johnson
after Budapest, Dallas, Memphis, Chicago
and Prague
there will be something
to be happy about
something to celebrate,
and from our houses
where the bird-claws of terror
keep scratching at the windowpanes,
from our insane, endless main streets,
our superb eight-lane expressways
where we can drive ourselves at sixty miles an hour
into misery,
from our boldly designed concrete bridges
that connect our garbage heaps,
from our lovely landscapes hidden
behind billboards advertising them,
from our forests wearing plastic rags,
our mountaintops wrapped in waxpaper,
and from our ocean
whose billions of hollow whitecap-teeth
fail to chew up not only the shit
from our oiltankers and factories
but even our old-fashioned and useless
rubber safes —
from everywhere
we might look at the moon and lick
our chops: we've screwed you too,
we've made you sweetheart just in time before
our rotting bed has collapsed under us.

Is there
something for me to celebrate?
The two daring astronauts
and Collins who is now circling above them
will be celebrated well when they return
to earth; and if they're wise enough
to retire, even in thirty years'
time they will have plenty on which to live
golden letters will list
their names in history books
and golden letters have a sheen of gold
assuming of course that in thirty years
there will still be books and history.

Hurrah for the crew, by all means!
But is there a captain,
who is the Aristarchos here,
the Columbus, the Wright, the Bleriot?
Hail, then, the creators
of rockets, including the pioneers,
the designers of V-2,
hosanna to all
who had tied rocket-wings
unto the ankles of thermonuclear
bombs to make them fly
from country to country
from planet to planet,
hosanna to all
who in the concrete bunkers of reactors
breed from the very excrement
of science
purple toadstools of destruction,
who manufacture and deliver freely
the hot spices of mustard gas to dress
our last bowls of salad, who recommend

our stone-age instincts white
phials of anthrax for a sedative,
who handed our chicken-brained leaders
the pushbutton of remote-control death
for something to play with,
and who, because the speed of our madness
is still far, far behind
the speedy wonders of technology,
equipped our asses with Niagaras
of solid-fuel propulsion,
hosanna to all
they celebrate along with us this evening
or rather permit us to celebrate them
modestly, as becomes mechanics
who do not work for glory
but for salaries and bonuses
paid out of public funds
who discreetly leave off
the word "military" before their titles
and whose lives
are guarded by plainclothes police, better
than my life or my cleaning lady's life
should we walk across Central Park at night —
they celebrate along with us this evening
except they know, this is no opening night
or even dress rehearsal, it is a bold leap
into the void; the rest is an attraction
for the clapping crowd, a circus act,
featuring the three astronauts
as the clowns of outer space.

The live coverage is over —
the newscasters explain
how Armstrong, Aldrin and Collins
will go in isolation once they're back

on earth for twenty days, in case
they picked up germs,
while our scientists will analyze
the lunar soil because they half expect
to solve the secrets of the universe
locked in these rocks — then some new commentators
praise the event by using the word Peace
as frequently as Cortez used to use
the name of Jesus Christ — do not believe them,
each sentence is a lie:
the ad-men of technocracy are cheating
they're lying, these chief engineers of death,
they know full well it is not on the moon
that there are germs; it is inside their heads
that both culture and science have become
a culture of germs,
they piss on the universe's secret
unless there is a government to buy it,
they piss on the rock samples of the moon
(whose Chief of Staff will spend money on rocks?)
they look for something else:
the bottom of a precipice or crater
on the lunar Sea of Tranquility
where they can put
a missile base, much more splendid than any
in Hitler's or Stalin's fondest dreams;
they will equip it fully in a few months
and aim it at one half of the earth,
then in a year or two some jaundiced,
lead-lipped and perspiring
Party leader
with the aid of a Lenin Prize or two
and a few bullets in the brain
will force a Soviet spacecraft into being
and a missile base in the Sea of Storms

aimed at the other half of the earth
and at us in the moon,
and from the moon we'll aim at them
on the moon
and from the earth we'll aim at them
on the moon
as we have aimed at each other on earth
mutually for some time,
and then we'll start all over once again
the game of the atomic bomb, new nations
land on the moon —

Enough!

the profile of von Braun comes on the screen
at a press conference, he's carefully
averting his eyes, perhaps he's afraid
his eyes will give away, but what is left
of him to give away?
He utters measured words, his jaw-line strong,
a classic nose, pure pleasure on his lips:
this man will never notice the dark
cape of werewolves around his own shoulders —
we have degenerated into instruments
in their hands helplessly; to swallow strychnine
may be a consolation but no defence against them,
nevertheless: no murderers have bored me
half so abysmally as they do,
these incarnations of the counter-human,
the schizophrenic gorilla
the cosmic gorilla
the suicidal gorilla
who has come to execute
the judgment of predestination
who is spilling on us
nature's ripe wine of fury
who shakes

our monstrous kind off the rim of the earth
whose patience has long been exhausted —
listen to Caesar, for he is victory
but he does not mean whatever he tells us
and he won't tell us whatever he means
he did conquer the moon
but did he notice her colour, her smell?
Listen to him no more
kick his loathsome television to pieces
his lunar lunacy
as the last act of a heritage of freedom
walk out into the garden, taste the trees
drink up the grass, run your fingers through
the moon's quicksilver hair.

Translated from the Hungarian
by George Jonas

HENRIKAS NAGYS

×

AUTUMN DREAM

A green-eyed girl comes through the foggy orchard.
Moonlight gleams off the old castle's copper turrets.
She offers me a handful of dead butterflies:
"Take them — the days of our sunny autumn.

In the evenings by the fireside when you open
your beloved book about *Le Grand Meaulnes*
who spent his dreams in roaming, they will blaze
with these butterflies in the bright hearth
and our autumn together will sigh up the chimney."

Translated from the Lithuanian
by Robert and Aldana Page

PASTORAL

Sons of the spit-turner strum guitars in the shadow:
translucent fingers pluck an old and mournful melody.
White steel airplanes dive through soundless space.

From beyond the lake comes the rasp of the sharpening scythe.

The withering trees of the orchard flounder in smoke and dust.
In the hot tar-spattered sand barefoot children
build castles and sing ditties.

From beyond the orchard comes the chirr of the sharpening scythe.

Vacant windows and rails gleam in the sun.
Airplanes flash in the blue like silver minnows.
Old guitars apathetically murmur through childish laughter.

From behind the hedge comes the close clang of the sharpening scythe.

Translated from the Lithuanian by
Robert and Aldana Page

FRAGMENTS OF CHILDHOOD

Strings of lifeless locomotives. Rusty rails in the fog.
The wind in the workyards sways tar-spattered dandelions.
Small dirty hands gather them and take them home.
Behind a smoky basement window an old woman smiles in her sleep.

Weeping women carry baskets of bleeding fruit
and cringe when the trains scream. Crowds of poplars
have gathered in the gully to bury the dead sun.
I listen to their dirge while awaiting father's return.

His red lantern swings far away in the night.
Heavy familiar steps! With a coarse sweaty hand
he strokes my hair . . . Beyond the river soldiers sing . . .
In the flaming doorway mother waits for us.
Quietly crackling, the night burns in the hearth.

Translated from the Lithuanian
by Robert and Aldana Page

WIND IN THE TREES

Birches

When the green rain falls on their lithe
and long and waving arms,
the spring wind flows;
and look: children are coming
along the lane, and suddenly they cannot
find their way home —
and they stand by the edge of the lane
and cry
and caress with tired hands
the delicate curls of one another's
bright heads.

Pines on the Seashore

In the evening sun, like flames —
your slender trunks.
In the evening wind you are alone,
alone on the moist sand

you wade into the sea and toss
needles into the surf.
And when night comes
and the waves grow weary
your black trunks
like great arms
rock the stars and sky.

Willows

An immense invisible hand —
how it tosses you, dusty willows!

You sway, you dip your branches
in the glimmering depths, and black
pond water — like blood — on your leaves
and on your damp bark flows back into the pool.

Mountain Ash

Like small drops of blood —
your fruit falls to the mud
under the falling rain . . .

And you stand alone here
by a little street and sadly
sway in the October rain.

Oaks

They are coming, a great, somber throng.
They slowly sway their heavy crowns,
and like distant thunder, like drums,
their song reverberates weirdly:

we carry the sky
we bear the bloody sky
we carry the dead sky
we bring the night

Their huge dark hands,
their clutching fingers twisted with wounds,
hold a rigid cloud
like a great black coffin.

They are coming. They carry the sunset,
slowly swaying, a great, somber throng.

Translated from the Lithuanian
by Robert and Aldana Page

APOCALYPSE

Pallid clouds drift above the ruins of the town.
In the shadow of the gray mountain gagged springs
gaze into the poisonous sky. The moon rises
from the clutch of charred elms into the cool
metallic expanse of the empty night.

This is the hour between life and nothing
when the heart is still and death has not yet come.
In the deep valley by the stream the nightingales
have ceased their celebration. The shadow of the well-lever's
cross falls athwart the pale marketplace.

The shattered gate of the ancient cemetery
hacks at the silent night in its weird lament.
The battered grass. The blackened cobbles. The embittered
earth-streaked faces of men. In the timeless light
of the full moon lie helmets full of yesterday's warm rain.

Translated from the Lithuanian
by Robert and Aldana Page

JOURNEY INTO THE NIGHT

The foreigner placed his hand on your shoulder
in the cool, late evening at the old harbor saloon.
Yellow sand and wine flowed in a thin stream
from glass to glass.

The drunk placed his blue hands on the dirty table
and wept. The nervous light of neon signs crawled across
his damp face when the tall foreigner's ivory hand
touched the shoulder of my tired friend.

Poets died in bars even before Villon and Poe,
drunk on green absinthe and cheap wine,
on the glare of harbor lights and the screams of boats
leaving the black pier for sun-lit journeys.

Young stallions romped in their dreams in endless pastures . . .
spotted trout danced in the crystal waterfalls of childhood
striving upstream to spawn and die . . . The pale boys
gathered shadows of slow clouds from the warm sand . . .

The foreigner laid his hand on your shoulder.
The scale of shadows is quivering in painful balance.
In the conical glass the stream of sand is accelerating, dwindling.
The only street is blind and leads to the empty pier.

Translated from the Lithuanian
by Robert and Aldana Page

TERRA INCOGNITO

In the land of blue snow there are no trees:
only the shadows of trees and the names of trees
written by a somber hermit in the writing of the blind.

In the hall of mirrors not a single person is left:
only profiles cut out by the cutter of Tilsit fair,
and silhouettes traced on the dusty glass by the fingers
of the dead violinist late in the evening of All Souls.

In the valley of the ebbing rivers there is no birthplace:
only long rows of barracks, wooden sphinxes
with their sooty heads on their paws, dreaming
of flags, summer, sun and sand.

In the land of blue snow only names remain,
lines and drawings and letters remain on ashes.
In the land of blue snow there is no land.

Translated from the Lithuanian
by Robert and Aldana Page

TULIN ERBAS

AS TENDER GIFTS

I plucked my flowers and tossed them
At the songs of waters
As tender gifts, as affection, as love.
My rains burst out,
My desert rains
Pouring on unlikely grounds,
As vineyards, as gardens, as steppes.

Translated from the Turkish
by the Author

WOMEN IN PARADISE

In paradise women thirsted for love
Where would they go?
Their sins could not be sized up
In thick volumes, where would they go?

How long will these spring showers
Keep coming down?
Women in the void, women in the void,
Worlds abandoned . . .

Translated from the Turkish
by the Author

GO TO SLEEP

He was alone, in the prayers of darkness,
Planets were beckoned, out of distant voices . . .
To have the fondest wish come true, to reach out,
Then to fall asleep again, the loveliest sleep.

I have placed you next to the summer flowers
Along aromas heavy, ripe, deep.
I have left you to beautiful dreams in eternity,
Go to sleep, plunge into the loveliest sleep.

Translated from the Turkish
by the Author

MERMAIDS

Chambers under sea
Are sealed off.
Closed to mermaids.
Poems are spent,
Chambers are locked . . .
The keys are lost
In the oceans . . .
Let them sleep where they lie,
The buccaneers are nearby.

Translated from the Turkish
by the Author

JULY IF YOU LIKE

I shall not return again
To the lilac dreams.
Don't wait on the road, hoping.
Turn back, don't even start out,
On October mornings,
Or July if you like.
Leave your drapes ajar
So the blues may enter.
There are no mirages any more,
Steep roads are straight now
And the stars awakened
From their morning sleep.
Don't wait on the road, alone.

Translated from the Turkish
by the Author

KEEP A KHAYYAM BEAUTY

Forget the black hair,
Keep a Khayyam beauty
This way . . .
The pupils of my eyes
Are the companions of solitude.
We cast away the hourglass
Along our minds.
Sand is for me
And solitude for you
This way . . .
The pupils of my eyes
Are the companions of solitude
In the hourglasses
This way . . .

Translated from the Turkish
by the Author

NICHOLAS CATANOY

10

New-yorking. Nights come east. For security reasons all dogs assume code names & Belches come from behind the eyes / bats circle (no matter what doors you might try to close) & This apple tastes like ESSO & One is obeyed by a dead whale & Neon toccatas and scars / as far as neighbors go / or rectal dialogues and their intricate meanings. Then, the reverse of seed / to witness a hanging & parrots barking & the statue of Liberty casually holding Xerxes' phallus.

14

The rivers wait as if struck by some icy thoughts / their eyes are at the day level & A blind hand / fixed upon spring. That's latitude.

18

All rocks emerge when a flower changes its voice & No part of us smells the color between two gestures.

23

The web has left the spider through dark / a tree sobs / someone is trying to pick my face from a slaughter-house. (We were all four turned to the north; the web, the tree, "someone" and me. As the birds on the hedge, wondering at the meaning). & Tell us who we are. And what happens next?

25

I am a tourist. I never slug, gurgle, hobnail or titilate. I
intend to stand in the middle of my stomach. I am your cacophony
but I mourn Einstein's last copulation. I flatter Monsieur Teste
and am afraid of my left fist (Ce que je vois m'aveugle. Ce que
j'entends m'assourdit. Ce en quoi je sais, cela me rend ignorant).
I count the essence of unspoken words. I turn on all the lights
and tremble. I am full of dead nightingales.

30

Bones seek their own deepness / before a tale is told & Flowers
meet the corpse or the bride & We are being called back & Who then
in us wanders?

33

My brain is a rock / thinking the end is not the end & But what
we dream is not what we get / such geology is just a comfortable
agony.

37

Your other face, behind the apple / the feeling in between / my
heart, — too soft to separate the moonlight from the skin & I
know your blood / another fake & et la morale d'aujourd'hui:
NEVER MISTAKE THE APPLE FOR THE SNAKE.

42

Mini-apocalypse / coconuts falling out like old teeth / leaving no
parts of the body untouched & What will you say with your last
breath? MEHR LICHT! like Goethe or shout three times: my foot!
my foot! my foot! to hide your fear.

49

Each wall, an open eye / I crawl & A lichen blinking in my blood, to size the sky & I grasp the midnight bell who killed a mocking-bird / and all the rest / and crawl and crawl and crawl.

60

Speech is a hole / the gospel, a little cough & I want to run both ways / but meditation is a fraud / a print of bare feet growing still and cold, (minus a nose) & A rooster's cry leaps back into my ribs / sinking somewhere, between the shade and rear.

Translated from the Rumanian
by the Author

CLEPSYDRA

Falling asleep, whirling,
Clepsydra with a swinging gait,
On the track of clavichord's tones
With lunar hands and ducky words.

Betting on heel's eyes
You've fooled us with gongs and frankincense.

Dividing yourself, in virgin moments,
And through the meditating earth,
Oh clever clew and nothingness with root,

Where is eternity? Where is the light?

Translated from the Rumanian
by the Author

WINTER INSTANT

The hand, with its distorted step
in the polar heart,
colder than a ghost,
storming the eyelids
heavy with nadir
between the icy flowers
in a stellar shrinkage
at my window
sick of white spasms.

Translated from the Rumanian
by the Author

AEGRI SOMNIA

Nights over silence's shoulder simulating
    the corrosive emptiness of the verain.
Nights with hoofs.
Nights of carnivorous absinth.
White nights.

White nights like the abyss of sextantes,
White nights like the laughter of a scarred hand,
White nights like a dead swan,
White nights like the Sunday lava of the birch-trees,
White nights like Borgia's rings,
White nights like an expaction in trinitroglycerine's
    sanctuary,
White nights like the hollow of the mirror,
White nights like the testimony of the lips of wax,
White nights like Horu's ashes,
White nights like the mimosa of the Arctic Circle,
White nights like the dagger of the empty subterraneans,
White nights like the blood of the lunar cuttlefishes.

White nights. White nights. White nights. . . .

Translated from the Rumanian
by the Author

TEXTES

1

The sky thrown at random. The decapitated head of Pan.
The half of an Alexandrine verse. My steps. The echo
of these semi-open doors. Vacuum's saliva, like a hall-
mark of Monades. The anchor perforating the eye filled
with memoirs and the comforting Requiem of hyenas.

Translated from the Rumanian
by the Author

TEXTES

6

Stars with tormented eyes narrating my own fiction. Somewhere a consumptive sun remains unchanged. I forgot how the heart looks like. Canine snow. Pupil's opaque mingled with the voice. Walking. And I am walking like a stranger in sleep, without witnesses, listening to my own demented hostage.

Translated from the Rumanian
by the Author

BOGDAN CZAYKOWSKI

THE COLLECTIVE

My steppes are coming to life again;
the plough turns up shrapnel.

My arid soil
upturned
is losing its livid hue.

We establish primitive irrigation.
We get out together to the fields.

The earth exacts many deaths
before black soil overlays the sand.

With a pitchfork I scatter the dung of the past.
My plough throws earth over a mouldering coffin.

I am tilling fallow land over destruction.
Digger of fields or graves?

Translated from the Polish
by Catherine Leach and Michael Bullock

ARS POETICA

Configurations are conspiracies.
Maturing is a matter of betrayals
and the recovery of innocence
and of the birds relentless
longing for migration.

There is the law of the four wheels
that do not overtake each other
and of the fifth wheel
that follows in the dust
purple and gold.

There is the law of the falling of ripe apples.

The law of reins.

Beyond self-betrayals
you must reach after flexibility.

But there is no consent to death.

Translated from the Polish
by Catherine Leach and Michael Bullock

AGE DE LA PIERRE

In this town the rubble has been cleared away.
New homes have been built
(You can see that for yourself).
The cemeteries have been tidied up.
The courts have sentenced the guilty, and then the others.
Later amnesties were bestowed upon the murdered
and rehabilitation upon those still left alive.
The voluntary exiles were permitted to return.
But they kept on hoping.
Some were swallowed up by profit.
Yet there was repatriation.
And here and there some did come back to life.
Others did not survive the miracle of Lazarus.
You ask, what vistas open up?
The rubble of the mind cannot be cleared, not even if you build
Monuments
On every grave.
Until new men appear.
Of whom we know only this:
Their heritage will be heavy.

Translated from the Polish
by Catherine Leach and Michael Bullock

AGE DE LA PIERRE (II)

We pick up broken pieces,
we strike fire from flint, clothe ourselves
in skins;
my husband has a beautiful igloo

a classic vista unrolls

we have cultural workers
and in general live on good terms with nature
the animals treat us as their kin
now birds sing to us
now butterflies flutter around us
my husband preserves in an iron box
a bow-tie with a diamond pin

we talk with the lord god
under the bare skies
and feel as though by the fire-place
the sun is shining
but there are lots of ashes
as once on a wednesday

children are born to us singing
like the fish in our rivers
and we think we are on the earth
or some other planet
or perhaps the moon

my youngest
is getting ready for an expedition
to Washington
apparently
thousands of books were microfilmed

in a shelter
Mona Lisa and Marilyn Monroe
and some bones
gleam whitely
left over from the days
when negroes resembled apes
and jews murdered christ

sometimes we dream of cities
Troy Athens Jerusalem London
but all that lies far back
before the man on the cross

a classic vista unrolls

here fawns are fawning
fraternal crocodiles
are digging over old kingdoms
out of the slime

loose ash is falling
and here and there smoke is still rising

Translated from the Polish
by Catherine Leach and Michael Bullock

GARDEN

for my mother

Here, in this garden, there certainly is a man.
But though many eyes are seen, they lack embodiment.
Here, in this garden, perhaps there is a woman:
A ripe breast lies amid glittering leaves.
And the whispering of leaves is like the hearing of a child —
As though a convolvulus were climbing sunflower stems.
Stealthily I brush aside grasses at someone's feet,
But still lack courage to raise my eyes:
Before me stands a nakedness: how beautiful it is here.
The garden's green arc took me into a quiet parenthesis
And covered the bright swelling with a banana leaf.
I rest my eyes and merely pluck
The crescent moon's bow-string — an arbitrary line.
I feel so satisfied with my construction in the blue
That the lightness of thought lifts the dome of distance,
Distinguishing a brilliant compass of the sky.
In this garden there certainly is a woman:
A white arm reclines upon an apple-tree,
While above, a fragmentary face still seeks completion,
And a man's naked torso emerges amid jasmine flowers.
Rustling in layers of leaves and leaves leaves leaves,
Rustling which kindles into a tall shape of flame
Green sparks of buds. The greenness of grass burns.
Night springs at the moon. A peacock slumbers beneath a star.
The wind gathers rusty silver. A palm whimpers over the wastes.
From a coconut shell a woman who certainly is here
Drinks milk. Her body is gilded
By the irreplaceable sun, then twilight chill combs
Her hair and heaps it, warm, over her shoulder.

So now I will come closer.
                                        Darkness rolls down the leaf.
Here was man — here is the hollow for his hip
Where now a furrowing wave chases leaves across a lake.
He probably placed these olives in the mouth into which flows
A briny drop — on his brow conceived —
A warm drop of sweat.
                                        So I will now retreat,
To measure the cactus shadow with the length of my sleep.
Quieta non movere. Let ants milk greenfly.
An axe clears the garden. Yet still the greenness burns
And the most beautiful silences still haunt the garden
Which once was called — and rightly so — hortus conclusus
Or paradise, lost, which here I have described
From memory.

Translated from the Polish
by Catherine Leach and Michael Bullock

THE EXPLICATION OF SURA

One lives in dreams
until torn apart
by dogs

dream visits are short
and the rest
is parting with dreams

crusades
crucifixions

I call you
and mutatis mutandis
I meet you in sleep

where one lingers
until torn to pieces
by dreams

First day of Spring, 1961.

Translated from the Polish
by Catherine Leach and Michael Bullock

EVENING SCENE

the claw of the sun
has scratched the clouds
till they bleed

with a moist tongue
the wind licks
their burning wounds

from the other side of the sky
through trees coagulating into dusk
creeps the moon-weasel

Translated from the Polish
by Catherine Leach and Michael Bullock

THE HOURGLASS

Holding the narrow neck of the hourglass
tight in my hand
I strive to return the sand
from the base.

I know that when it tightens
and when breath grows short
hosts of oxygen wait ready in the sky.
Crying in their sleep
birds announce dawn.

Wrung through the eye of the needle
I stand on its point.

I reverse the hourglass:
time grows eloquent once more.

Translated from the Polish
by Catherine Leach and Michael Bullock

MAN AND THE WHALE

Jonah spewed out by the whale
first washes himself,
though he loathes water.
Then he smoothes out his crumpled face
and goes to the ballet,
or to have one on the rocks.

The whale
makes off into the deep
shivering all over.

Translated from the Polish
by Catherine Leach and Michael Bullock

JOSE EMILIO PACHECO

VAINGLORY OR PRAISE IN ONE'S OWN MOUTH

By manipulation   By force   Relentlessly
          Or without pausing or hurrying
I have won a place forever
          To the left of zero
Absolute zero   The roundest
          most insurmountable   slippery zero
I procured a fine position in the other queue
          next to the emigrants expelled
from posterity
          And that is history

Translated from the Spanish
by George McWhirter

DIFFICULTIES IN SPEAKING THE TRUTH

Dutifully they practise love.
They forge verses from fire and dispatch
them to their recipients at the convent
And when the Holy Inquisition intercepts them
they talk about the rising from the dead
and the mystical union
between Christ and his Church

Translated from the Spanish
by George McWhirter

HIGH TREASON

I don't love my motherland. Its abstract brilliance
is ungraspable.
But (bad as it may sound) I'd give my life
for ten of its places: certain people,
ports, pine woods, fortresses,
a ruined city — grey, monstrous —
several figures in its history,
mountains
(and three or four rivers).

Translated from the Spanish
by George McWhirter

SCORPIONS

The scorpion attracts its mate
and welded together by the sting they observe
each other for one sullen day and night
and at the conclusion
of the nuptual encounter:
the male succumbs
and is devoured by the female
— which (says the preacher)
is more bitter than death.

Translated from the Spanish
by George McWhirter

WALTER BAUER

LEAVING THE APARTMENT

There will be no more parties in these rooms,
they are empty,
conversations have stopped for good.
The knock on the door is
no longer for me,
there are patches on the wall
where pictures hung,
most things were thrown in the garbage
without indulgence.
There will be no further exchange of tenderness,
a final line was drawn —
was the hand really quite steady?
My passport has a stamp
which it took me endless trouble to get —
the earth, which belongs to no-one, is now carefully laid out.
The door is open.
But what is behind the door?

Translated from the German
by Henry Beissel

EMIGRANTS

They came from San Cataldo,
from Racalmuto, Villa San Giovanni,
they had escaped from Sicily's African sun
and from perpetual poverty.
They sat on deck the "Argentina"
as if by the well in their village and chatted
as though there were no ocean
nor, after their arrival,
all those speechless things
like the Atlantic even colder than this.
The boat was for them a slowly moving
San Cataldo or wherever it was they came from
with their beggarly boxes.
Looking into their eyes you could see
tremendous kinds of hope:
Studebaker or Buick,
refrigerator, radio, a house,
and enough to eat always.
Some of the young men walked
with a sway of the hip
as if they had conquered Montreal (which none of them knew)
or all the gold-mines of the north.
And like a messianic pronouncement
one word was heard again and again:
money.

Translated from the German
by Henry Beissel

FROM SEVEN AT NIGHT TILL FOUR IN THE MORNING

From seven at night till four in the morning
I clean leftovers from plates and dishes
Into the garbage can,
Wipe glasses, silver plates, cutlery.
At nine my dreams are still fresh and shiny
And I could make the world a better place.
At midnight time drags itself across the steamed-up room
And lies down to die at my feet.
At two I hardly remember anything
And wipe the leftovers of my life
Into the garbage can.
At three I clean up the kitchen till it shines
In odourless light.
At four I step into the sharp lonely wind
And before the Milky Way fades
I drink from it my freedom.

Translated from the German
by Henry Beissel

THIS IS THE HOUR FOR THE DRUNK TO SLEEP

This is the hour for the drunk to sleep
Struck by the hammer of intoxication —
Look at him lying there, dull clay in God's image.
This is the hour when men and women sleep
Gutted by the lightning of lust —
Look at the satiate, whispering flesh: image of God.
This is the hour when the condemned wait
To walk to the gallows or the gas chambers —
Watch them take step after step on a path
Not green, not earthy, not remembering —
Watch them travel from the past to nothingness: God's image.
This is the hour when bank safes are opened
And shadows slip away like mice in the grass: God's image.
This is the hour when suicides take leave of a world
That served them an incomprehensible mixture of too little or too
much —
Listen to the stillness, the leap, the tightening of the noose,
the last precious breath.
Farewell, image of God.
This is the hour when I clean up the kitchen in empty silence
And rise finally with a look of exhaustion and the satisfaction
of sweat.
I too, I too God's image.

Translated from the German
by Henry Beissel

A MIDWIFE SPEAKS

I have been here often, this is where children are always born —
sometimes at night —
or when life offers a woman the cup
that tastes terribly bitter
between birth and death.

When the bell shatters my dreams
I know somewhere the time has come
and quickly I comb back my sleep.
Downstairs someone is already waiting for me to come.

It is always the same: a strange room
smelling of unborn life, of sweat,
of fear, of the inability to give birth yet, and of urine.
Here is a clock and there a table,
a plate with food, upon a pillow
the hollow of a face covered with night.

The time has not come yet, I have prepared everything.
Human beings are waiting here at night for the arrival of
    another human.
But it's an arrival amidst blood and slime.

How many rooms there are — and all like this:
mildew on the walls, many beds
or the equivalent of beds, up above the plaster falling off.
In each one: smells. In each one: people.
I hear the house exhale.
Whispers in the plumbing: the lavatory.

Ghost of this house, who makes me shudder —
and here: the body's cell in ferment.
A scream. It is the same scream everywhere.
And above each one, mountains of night and womb.

And a tiny voice screams at the house
and at the night
which will become closer yet.

Translated from the German
by Henry Beissel

THE PAPER-BOY

In the first morning light
the paper-boy threw
the news of the world
Against closed doors.
The early light accompanied him
Like a silent, obedient dog —
But he did not see it, he was working
Distributing world.
Only after the last bundle
Made up of the waste of yesterday
was thrown away with a practised but indifferent hand,
Did he become aware of his loyal companion.
Whistling, the boy rode his cycle home.
The morning ran alongside,
A golden, barking dog.

Translated from the German
by Henry Beissel

THIS WAS NOT THE WAY MEN SCREAMED

This was not the way men screamed in front of our trenches,
I have never heard any human being scream like this,
We could no longer shut it out, incessantly
We had to listen:
I believe it was the earth itself screaming, deeply wounded,
Or perhaps it was the wailing of the injured stars.
I crawled out into the dusk
To release the screaming horse with a bullet.
It grew still then, the world
Seemed world again in the slowly fading light.
Those in the forest across from us must have been glad too
Because their ears too must have got more than their fill.
Then there was a shot, and at once it was inside me —
Simply a blow, like a hand that flings open
A door into dark adjacent rooms.
I groaned a little, but not for long.
Today night came quickly in deep silence
And with great coolness at its fiery core.
Nobody came to get me.

Translated from the German
by Henry Beissel

GUTTORMUR J. GUTTORMSSON

THESE BONES WERE WAGES

The canine and his master,
Hungry wandered they,
Facing grim disaster,
Having lost their way.

The master, faint and fearful,
Lay down upon the trail.
The quadruped, more cheerful,
Looked on and wagged his tail.

The sight caused cerebration;
He saw a remedy:
He severed with elation
The dog's extremity.

His relish to inspire,
And flavor to enhance,
He fried the tail entire,
Suspended from a branch.

And having gnawed the flesh,
The master could afford
His canine to refresh
With the bones as a reward.

Translated from the Icelandic
by Thorvaldur Johnson

SAMAR ATTAR

CITY OF THE THOUSAND WOUNDS

Will the rain wash your dusty face
O city of thousand wounds
And will the hidden prince
Ride again these narrow lanes?

. . .

Our garden is full of weeds
Our hands stained with blood
Where should we start
Binding up the branches
Cutting back the sprigs?

. . .

Mirrors float on the water
But like some shooting stars
They fall in the bottom of the sea.
Ah how our backs ache
We the elderly
The cursed.

. . .

We have no names, no titles
Our mosques are deserted
O city without pigeons
Where can I hide my face?

. . .

Those broken minarets
Are covered with grayish dust

Shall we shine the edges
With our aprons
With our shawls?

. . .

Ah don't you see his face
Looming through the ruins?
Don't you hear the leaves
Falling on the ground?
Let us shine the edges
Let us shine.

. . .

The rats are coming
We see them in every corner
Spinning around and falling
Their mouth is open
Their fur is wet
O city of rats
Where is the air, the air?

. . .

Vipers in the land
Vipers in the pool
Who will pluck me a rose?
Who will find me a hiding place?
Wash me my sister
I smell of a carrion
Cold, cold my bones.

. . .

Pray you, a word or two before you go
Do not say . . .
Ah what is the use?

We have no tale
No deeds, no history
To be told
But you must not speak
For out of our sorrows
We will rise again
Wipe off the dust
Wash all the windows

. . .

Drown, drown my sister
Your bed is made of daisies
And in the glassy stream
We'll wash the garments
Shine the rings
And here at the shore
I will wait for you
And sing.

Translated from the Arabic
by Gwendolyn MacEwen

THE FAIR

"I've seen children
In the bottom of the sea
Their note-books were smeared with blood
Their eye-lids wet with tears."
O mon amour, mon frère
What does a clown see?
He shouts, he laughs, he sings
But when the curtain falls
He only weeps.

. . .

Once I walked in the bazaar
It was a warm lovely day.
"Senorita, do you care
For a kettle
Or perhaps
A vase?"
I did not know what to say
And what if I stopped by Monsieur Légère
Bought a head-piece from the Promised Land
Ah mon amour, mon amour
Is Lawrence here in a cage?
What if I bought the man
Wouldn't it be nice for the stage
After all, he is just a man
Wasn't it the desert he wrote about
And that barbaric race?

. . .

Those kids you talk about
Are being displayed in our fair.
Mon amour, mon frère
Do I care, you ask, do I care
The buyer and the seller do not really care.
But there was no blood as you say
It was a clean game, I believe, a very clean game!

. . .

"Mesdames et Messieurs
Les plus belles marchandises
Venez, venez
Des antiquités
D'Asie et d'Afrique."
And what if I stopped by Monsieur Légère
Bought a head-piece from the Promised Land
There is still time
And the girls are busy with the guys
Come on Nadine, there is still time.

. . .

"Des enfants, des enfants surtour . . .
Dora, ai-je rêvé, il m'a semblé
Que les cloches sonnaient à ce moment-là?"[1]
And what do you call me Dora for?
It is the jingling of the fair's bells
I cannot hear your voice
What a nightmare!
Keep your mirror please
I think I know my face
And above all do not use foreign words
I do not understand this French of yours.

. . .

[1]Albert Camus, *Les Justes,* (Paris, 1950) pp. 72-74.

What a fool. He likes to call me names
I do not pretend to be a Spanish Knight
Fighting against the wind.
I have chosen to live
Wearing a monkey's mask
And after all why should he ask me
Whether I like the waves?
Ah, it is absurd
I don't understand what he means.

. . .

I never said no
I always played the role of the clown
And in the fair
Like a pipe
They would play upon me
But you know
I am well conversed in politics
By the way, have you heard the term
"Necessity of History?"
"Garçon, give me the bill
Monsieur, avec plaisir."

. . .

O mon amour, mon frère
What shall I do,
What shall I ever do?
Those kids of yours
Are being displayed in our fair
Bought and sold
And when I see their sad faces
I turn my face
Is it the wheel of fortune as you say?
And what if I tore the mask

And learnt how to say:
        No
        No
        No
        No
And sailed
O mon amour, mon frère
I wish I could sail.

Translated from the Arabic
by Gwendolyn MacEwen

THE SEER

Your hair was tousled
and your buttons all undone,
like children we ran
and panted in the waves
and played with sand.
But I heard you wailing,
a corpse was floating
on the face of the sea.
I said nothing,
I was panting after you like a faithful dog.
(Your hair, O your tinted hair,
how it excited me!).
We knocked at every door, but who would answer,
who would answer?
The shore was a graveyard
and the storm played with the grass
with your hair, with your black dress.
I saw the line of your legs,
I saw the shadows.
Stones rattled against the doors
and you broke into tears.

. . .

An old man peered out from an antique door
carrying a candle,
his hut was a night of sorrow
and he waved, but you wept.
"You — black-wrapped woman,
why are you weeping?"
the old man asked
and blew out the candle.

There were five in a boat
and my love Omar was one.
"Ssh, don't speak his name!"
the old man said.
Two days I waited for the tide
but the boat never came.
A seer told me
          the boat went down,
and five were drowned, and Omar was one.
"Sssh, I told you not to speak his name!"
Why, why? you wailed,
as your red hair billowed,
strand by strand.
"In our village when a man dies
swallowed by waves,
we don't mention his name.
Here a man dies the death of a fly,
the women don't wear black
and no one cries.
So is it with those five.
You, black-wrapped woman,
please leave my hut,
you have the devil's touch."
The open door creaked
and outside the wind was singing.

. . .

"Shall we go to the forest?"
I asked, but you didn't reply.
"I'm a seer, a Greek seer,
aren't I, aren't I?"
The black shawl was swinging
in the wind, was swinging.
Waves were swallowing the boat
with five men within.

(Your hair, O your tinted hair,
how it excited me!).
Shall we go to the forest?
Black-wrapped woman,
what's wrong with you?
He's dead, he's dead, he's dead!
Can't you hear the wind moaning,
can't you hear?

. . .

In a corner of the town
I saw you fleeing.
Was it from me you fled?

Translated from the Arabic
by Gwendolyn MacEwen

MANUEL BETANZOS-SANTOS

FOUR POEMS

the early light of night
was broken
          and the harmony of your round arm

when a total and enemy light
followed
          after our dreams
              and wounded the rhythm of day

. . .

let us go and get lost in the white forest of Sweden
in search of love let's go

while the copper in the air absorbs the silence

while you
while you my king hand out helmets

to everyone and pass around with your ring
revenge and war.

. . .

as the skeleton of winter
          grasps the tree
so man's white skeleton
peers
          through your proud flesh

the earth's green face now
barely clothes the shape
of her poor skull
          moulded by future guns.

. . .

through the clay of your silence
let me recall you again

though the clay is like time
and you   always   silence

Translated from the Spanish
by the Author

SOMETIMES LOOKING

Sometimes looking at a tree we see a face

sometimes it turns out that not every man
has a house or a country

sometimes there is no understanding and words
have a terrible and limitless power

Rewarded be those who suffer for theirs
is the surest and most inhuman death

and sorrow is parallel to injustice.

Sometimes looking at a tree we realize
what is the reverse of life

and looking
and feeling
life

blessed be those who speak the truth
and do not fear to speak it always.

Translated from the Spanish
by the Author

THE PLANET

Once upon a time they came from another country
and in their hunger ate up the children of the blind
and wicked king.

The next day the king smashed his crown.
The next day the king killed his wives.
The next day the king had a vision
that there were only skeletons in his kingdom.

The next day a nameless planet appeared in the sky
and flowers, rivers, and mountains began to come out.

The next day the king died of remorse.

Translated from the Spanish
by the Author

IF I WERE A RIVER

If I were a river
I would make a people, a sea, or a mountain.

There would be an end to all the miseries
of the earth.

If I were a river.

Then the sea said to the mountain
if I were a river
and the mountain said to the sea
it would be mine.

If I were a river,
I would make neither seas nor mountains.

I would make a people.

Translated from the Spanish
by the Author

SONG OF THE CHILD AT THE WINDOW

Child, don't lie down among the leaves
and give me the small bird
you hold imprisoned in your hands.

Look at the trees moving.
Not at the lilacs falling.

Child, in the green lilac leaves.

The distant autumns returning
that bow the breast
and blanch the head.

Child, don't lie down among the leaves.

Translated from the Spanish
by the Author

POEMS OF INDIFFERENT WAR

Flower lashed by the wind.
The sun has hammered you.

Shaken by night.
Slashed by the early rain of morning.

The boot of the soldier eager for horizons
has crushed you.

The weight of the heavy tanks stops short.

Mute, you smile, you look, and again you smile.
A presence coming to meet you.

Man does not want to kill you.

You can communicate your spirit to him.
He may be saved.

A presence.
An absence.

The soldier can die, with you.

Translated from the Spanish
by the Author

RACHEL H. KORN

THE HOUSEMAID

The orchards of her home
still blossom in her glances
and in her dreams great flocks
of geese are feathered;
she used to drive baby geese
to the pond every spring
and guard them from the
crows and owls but now
for days she walks around
bewildered and her whole
body greedily drinks in
the fragrance from the new cut
wood piled up by the stove
ready for burning.

Her faraway home was so
beautiful but it was a small
farm poor and rocky and
there were seven mouths
to feed so she the oldest
came to the city and here
her two hands are now the oars
which row her life through
dark and steamy kitchens.

When she gets a letter
from the neighbor's son
she runs to strangers
hanging on their glances,
first she reads their faces
for goodwill then begs them
quietly to read her letter,

to tell her all they
must tell all all that
he has written! Then she
sees their scornful smiles
at his loutish crudely formed
letters which for her contain
the alphabet of love,
and she blushes, hides her face
for shame.

All week long her heart
composes answers until
at last it's Sunday and
the words are put down
beside each other like
invalids on pink paper
decorated with doves
and wreaths of roses.
Her girl friend scribbles
the words in a hurry then
reads out whatever was
dictated ending with
kisses and respectfully
yours; she smiles fleetingly
and in the corners of her mouth
lurk the shy love words
she has nursed all week
and there they hover
captive and unspoken.

Sometimes in an hour of rest
she opens her old prayer book
with a gold cross embossed
on its black cover; with awkward
hands she caresses the strange
letters, words full of God

and love and mercy and her eyes
grow dreamy thinking about
the miraculous world of A B C.

The world she knows
is tied in a thousand knots,
even the world of her prayer book
with its circles and lassos
is like some Judas: treacherous:
ready to sell her in a minute
for thirty hard days
of labor in every month.

Translated from the Yiddish
by Miriam Waddington

ROBERT ZEND

ARABELLA

For Irene

Even now Arabella continues to wake up at seven in the morning
walks into the kitchen and checks to see that everything is in order
she stops to stare through the window at the trees in the garden
her son and daughter leave for school without a hello or good-bye

When she turns to their bird it beats its wings in fright
when she pats their dog it whimpers and runs for cover
their cat however ignores her and passes by unfeelingly
in their aquarium their goldfish splash on indifferently

She is used to the fact that nothing stares back at her from the mirror
but she finds curious the sensation of playing the piano soundlessly
when their new mother washes her little girl's hair before bedtime
she abruptly turns her back on them under her photograph on the wall

At times she flees the house and rides on roofs of trains
or walks through walls to view some strange new families
or shows up at school to help her son when he needs it
but evenings find her at the table where no one set a plate for her

In bed she feels no jealousy when her husband makes love to someone else
but it always annoys her when some guest walks right through her
and at times like these she pouts and flicks out a lightbulb
or for an instant shorts the electric in the grandfather clock

Arabella knows she can remain with them for some time to come
until that voice that ancient powerful voice shall speak to her
shall sweep her up while everything else sinks down
and the rooms of the house like leaves in autumn shrivel and fall

This voice raises her and extends her and quickens her growth
it pulls the stopper from the bottle and opens up the empty spaces to her
and the compressed world that is contained within the bottle
is little more than a memory and the faintest of memories at that

But until then she continues to rise at seven
and peer into every corner and silently play the piano
and become cross with her children for not greeting her in the morning
and sweep across the sky racing the swallows in her odd anxious moments

Translated from the Hungarian
by John Robert Colombo

TISSUES

I

The time will come
when there will be no time
only electronic circuits
and I will remember
what the dead have forgotten
what the unborn have planned

II

By the way there's no certainty

III

If this holds true
of the upper reaches of consciousness
it applies down here too
so I barely exist
and whoever does exist is not me
might know vaguely about me
sometimes maybe

IV

A poem is a tunnel from a prison
for men who are about to die
the moon is full

V

I trust this transition won't hurt
but if it does I'll give it all my attention

VI

Can't you see I'm tossing and turning
why don't you take me by the shoulders and shake me
my mother my lover my god my self my all in one
a mix-up of names in the logic of this dream
it's important that you wake me up
I might even quarrel with you at the breakfast table
and complain that you think only of eating

VII

Yes of course I'm just an orange on a plate
how could I forget?

Translated from the Hungarian
by John Robert Colombo

BEFORE ASCENDING

Looking back he still saw
their little offices, where they scribble with important frowns,
their workshops, where they labour mightily on tiny things,
scar-faced gangsters, industriously rattling away at their machine guns
soldiers heaving hand-grenades with religious fervour,
priests directing the traffic up and down with formidable faces,
heads of families slaving to help what they couldn't have,
nudists trying to take pleasure in what no longer gave pleasure,
film producers inventing things and then believing in them,
capitalists piling up their money while they live in misery,
Communists acting as midwives to the future while murdering the present,
statesmen embracing the people in order to pick their pockets
the better,
assassins dead sure they are redirecting the river of time
mothers whose eyes are lost in their little babies' eyes,
scientists in need of a lifetime to dissect a single human hair,
poets delighting in their own feverish stutters and expecting others
to do the same,
lovers with eyes gone in each other's gaze . . .
seeing once again their specific spasms were all the same
taken in such dead earnest,
seeing again their large, cube-shaped buildings composed of small,
cube-shaped rooms,
their cities like anthills, their mechanisms
meticulously put together for crossing land, water, and air,
their toys through which they talk to one another in far-away places,
their lenses through which they look close or far or distortedly,
their thinking machines which they are not able to invent but
only imitate
and he remembers
that a second ago — it now seems a thousand years ago —

he himself was one among them —
how incredible, impossible, improbable —
he promises someone that he will give him the sign —
but he can't remember now to whom
or why —
the whole thing starts to drift apart, pull away,
the way colours on a palette run together,
the way a chunk of meat lacerates in the stomach,
the way a dream vanishes when the alarm-clock goes off,
he smiles and waves his hand,
his waking mind begins to remember,
he rubs his eyes, stretches, turns around,
and looks ahead.

Translated from the Hungarian
by John Robert Colombo

REQUIESCAT

The tiny wristwatch stopped ticking
and died and grew as cold
as cuff-links and tie-pins and rings and bracelets
and necklaces and earrings and brooches and diadems

Translated from the Hungarian
by John Robert Colombo

AFTER THAT

And after that he never went out in the evening to buy the milk
and bread his wife forgot to buy during the day
he never bothered to laugh at the jokes he heard, nor did he
bother to tell his own to make others laugh
nor did he take pen or pencil in hand to write poems, nor did he
type them out, nor did he feel like writing them at all
he did not go to work, he did not return from work, on Saturdays
he did not sleep in until noon, on Sundays he did not
have his afternoon nap for half an hour
he did not read books, did not play chess, did not cry, did not
swim, did not take photographs, did not enjoy music,
did not go to the movies
for he had no eyes, no hands, no tears, no ears, no legs, no heart,
no brain with which to do these things
they slowly dispersed in every direction farther and farther away
the way a pebble thrown into a pond creates concentric
circles

Translated from the Hungarian
by John Robert Colombo

WHEN

Death doesn't
end life
death just
interrupts it

a bookmark between page 256 and 257
a dental appointment on Friday at two
guests tonight
a movie tomorrow evening
a discussion that didn't end
coffee percolating on the stove
six shirts at the laundry
a holiday in Mexico this winter

this is what things are like
when a period is placed
in the middle of a sentence

Translated from the Hungarian
by John Robert Colombo

MORE AND MORE

For twenty-eight days the ovum wanders,
then it falls like a leaf in autumn —
is that all?
More.
Let there be one more, ten more, until . . .

Two cells have merged into one.
Should it stay one? No. More.
Let there be two, four, eight, and even more.

A child. It appears. Is that all?
It needs food. More. Must grow. More.
It matures. Does it stop there? Is that enough?
An only child? More.
Mankind can't die out in our generation.
More. And more.

We eat bread. Drink water. More.
We eat cake. Drink champagne. More.
We eat a worker. Ten workers. A hundred. More.
We eat a factory. Two factories. Five. More.
We eat countries. Oceans. Atmospheres. The earth is ours.
More.
The Moon. Mars. Venus. Does that satisfy us?
Not enough. More and more.

We make love. Once? More than once.
Twice. Twenty times. More. Five hundred times.
That's enough. But one woman isn't enough.
Two? Five? Ten? More and more.

We can read and write. More.
We know how to add. More.
We wrote one or two masterpieces. More.

We read a book. A library of books. More.
We can do calculus. More.
We can transplant hearts, devise artificial brains,
 blast off rockets
More and more and more.

From the cells of our bodies one word comes: More.
The sun's rays bombard the earth
and sprout plants all over it. More. Unicellular beings. More.
Fish. More. Reptiles. More. Mammals. More.
Man.
That's not the end. More and more.

Every single second, suns pulsate and pour
tons of energy on their planets,
and energy means but one thing: More.

Hasn't the universe been exploding long enough?
No, not long enough? More.

Death, and what can follow death? More.
Should we buy a second house? More.
After our world tour, should we travel again? More.
When this poem is finished, should I write another? More.
The sun orders us: More. From the core of the galaxy
 of galaxie
a telegram comes to ours
which is forwarded down to earth,
and when we read it, it says: More.

No other message.
No other meaning.
No other answer.

Only this one word message, meaning, answer,
which translates into human speech:
More!

Translated from the Hungarian
by John Robert Colombo

LITERARY CRITICISM

For Professor J. A. Molinaro

Leibnitz thought
this is the best
of all possible worlds

Voltaire thought
Leibnitz was wrong when he thought
this is the best
of all possible worlds

Pirandello thought
Voltaire was wrong when he thought
Leibnitz was wrong when he thought
this is the best
of all possible worlds

I think . . . but I'm wrong anyway

Translated from the Hungarian
by John Robert Colombo

MONDAY

It took me decades
to learn
the basic principles
of wisdom

This is this
Now is now
Here is here
I am I

Nothing else is true
there are no harps in heaven
there are no turtles holding up the world
the best investment is a t-bone steak

Translated from the Hungarian
by John Robert Colombo

SEVEN MINUTES

I'm sitting comfortably on the chesterfield in Vivian's apartment,
there are purple drapes and velvet curtains here and there,
there are classical paintings and baroque statues everywhere,
we converse in our sophisticated way, and she expects her husband
to arrive any moment now, he is expected within the hour.
In the middle of my sentence about
the Coptic art of Ethiopia, I notice
that her skirt had worked its way up over her pretty knees
revealing her well-formed, slender
thighs, and at the same time
I notice that her lips are trembling —
is it possible there's something still alive in her
that dates back to the time when, on the stairway,
I kissed her so wildly I bruised her lips?
I ask myself this — forgetting how
to complete the other half of my sentence on Coptic art,
loosing myself in her eyes until she casts them down
and begins to mumble about her husband and how much she loves him.
Feeling awkward, I get up and go over to the window
and pull aside the heavy drapes
so I can see the six other apartment houses,
one behind the other in battle-array. But the six
are not there now, now there's only
emptiness there, nothing else.
I peer out and look down:
the wall of the building drops vertically to the ground,
and the ground continues dropping down, vertically and steeply,
as if the earth itself had been split in two:
there is nothing in front of me, nothing.
I let the drapes fall so Vivian
won't see what I see and won't worry.

I step over to the bookshelf, select a book and start reading aloud
her favourite poem, but when I turn the page,
the poem doesn't continue, there's only a blank page,
and blank page follows blank page to the end,
I shut the book.
"And so on," I manage to say, "you know the rest,"
and sit back on the sofa beside her.
I draw on my cigarette but it has gone out half-smoked.
I pick up the telephone to make certain
what I know in advance,
that I won't hear the usual hum
because the line is deaf and dumb.
I don't want to tell her, I don't want her to get nervous.
"Really, my husband should arrive any moment now,"
she slurs her words in embarrassment, but I know
that he won't come home ever again.
"Do stay and have dinner with us," she says.
"Alright," I reply, and I know
that the dinner will never be served.
"Vivian, do you know that should the sun explode,
it would kill all life on earth and bring everything to a halt,
but that this would not happen for eight minutes
after the explosion — that's how long it takes
for the light and the electromagnetic waves
or, if you prefer, for the message
to arrive here from the sun?
The fastest thing in the world is the speed of light,
and during those eight minutes
everything would live on in the same way . . . "
She purses her lips and frowns,
"I know all that, but why bother me with it now?"
she asks, but I don't tell her why.

Translated from the Hungarian
by John Robert Colombo

SENSELESS STORY

for John Robert Colombo

Feeling fine, I lean back in my easy chair, finally caught up
The last letter is all-but finished, all I have to do is find the right
adjective in the third line from the bottom
I have to drop it in the mail today so that the official in charge
at the head office will get it tomorrow
It's an extremely important report on a machine manufactured in a
Far Eastern country
If we decide to buy it, our production will increase ten-fold and our
little firm will ease all competition right out of the market
Then within the next twelve months we will become a great international
combine
The last mail pick-up is at five, it's only three now, so I have plenty
of time to go down
And have a cup of coffee, then in fifteen minutes I can come back and
will have no trouble at all finding the right adjective
Hatless, I take the stairs two at a time, February sounds like a
rabid dog howling in the streets
Pasted on the door of the little restaurant where I usually have coffee
there's a sign
which reads "REOPENING SOON" but I don't feel like returning without
my coffee
My saliva glands are working overtime, I turn up the collar of my
jacket and run three blocks over to the next restaurant
It's crowded, every table's full, except for one chair at one table
at which a beautiful blonde sits
She smiles and offers me a seat, I sit down, her eyes are like moons
wandering among clouds, her voice is velvet-soft
Policemen burst into the place, look around quickly, spot her, head
for her, start to rough her up

"I am not what you think I am," she tells them quietly, with dignity,
and pointing at me she says, "Ask my husband"
"Is she telling the truth?" the policemen with the red face asks,
I nod, he salutes and the bank of policemen leaves as quickly
as it came
We leave together too, arm in arm, but down the street we see them
tailing us, so slowly we walk across the city
I ask her whom they thought she was, she doesn't know, but what's
important is that we pulled through
We apparently live in a three-story apartment house at the edge of
the city, our flat is on the third floor and the elevator is
out of order
We walk up the spiral staircase and at every landing we stop to kiss
each other
"I've the feeling I've known you for a long time,' I gasp, and she
bursts out laughing, and says, "How poetic that is!"
"I can't imagine there'll ever be a time when we won't kiss on stair-
cases," I say, but she waves her hand and says, "I know you . . .
What about the usher in the movie theatre last month?" she asks, and
her eyes grow hard with hate
"How do you know about that?" I grow alarmed, "last month we didn't
even know . . . " but by now we're there
In the flat the cleaning lady is waiting for me to pay her, she
addresses me by my given name, I look at her with surprise
Good Lord this is my mother who died when I was only a child, but she
puts her finger to her lips to tell me not to say anything
Maybe then it's possible that my father's alive too? I want to walk
out into the hall with her but my wife calls me back angrily
"Now you're even flirting with cleaning ladies! Warm up some milk
for the child"
I don't dare ask what child, but then a child toddles into the room,
and he's really my son
We put him to bed, then we eat supper, old friends come over afterwards
to play cards

The heat is unbearable, I offer to go out to get some ice cream, and
our company enthusiastically agrees
I bump into the mailman at the front entrance, "I'm lucky today," he
says, "you saved me some stairs to climb"
he hands me a telegram, I rip it open and read it: "In the harbour
tonight at eight"
Who in the world sent this, I wonder, but then I start to remember,
Alex and Jack and the old gang a week ago we agreed that we would
meet this Wednesday
Maybe the shipment of new tombstones from old cemeteries has arrived
from Albania, we ordered them months ago
I grab a cab and we speed to the harbour, but the driver suddenly
slams down the brakes
He pulls a gun on me, I put up my hands, he hits me with the butt of
his pistol, I faint
I wake up, under me there's the shaking rocking bottom of a boat
among sacks and ropes
For eleven days I toss and turn, they give me nothing to eat or drink,
they don't even open the hold, I hammer in vain
Half-dead having nightmares, blinding beams of flashlights wake me up
quick hands grab me and dress me
At the prow of the ship a committee of elegantly attired government
officials speaks an unknown language to me, a band plays music
The officials take me to their parliament, their king shakes my hand,
their dinner in my honour consists of fifteen courses
They praise me, present me with a diploma with ribbons usher me into
a theatre
The first performance of my play is being offered that evening it's an
amazing experience to hear
My words recited in another language, the actors are excellent in
their parts
The leading lady clings to me, accompanies me up the elevator to the
penthouse apartment I live in
Servants butlers interpreters surround me, the king wants me to visit
him daily

I want to return home but newsboys wander up and down the streets
shouting "Heir-Apparent Assassinated," "New World War"
For four years I stay, meanwhile I enjoy success after success, I even
receive a letter from a former friend
Once ten years ago when I was starving I wrote him a letter but he
didn't answer, now he's starving so I don't answer
One bright day a helicopter lands on the lawn in front of my house
while I am busy in my observation dome observing the ring of
Jupiter
"We may go now," the pilot says, I get in and the jet plane swoops
over the ocean
I arrive, I head for the old street where my wife and child lived on,
but no one knows about them
My closest cousin doesn't recognize me, asks me for my identification
papers then asks me to forgive him
He faintly remembers knowing a relative with my name, but this
relative fell from the third floor when he was a child, was
a wheelchair case for a year until he died
I remember too, the wheelchair but nothing else, I ask about my
mother, he directs me to the cemetery,
I roam among the tombstones but I don't find the right one, the
caretaker says, "Albanian smugglers stole it"
Then something flits through my mind, something I seem to have
forgotten ages ago
I walk towards my office, who knows what's happened to it, the older
people have surely all died, the new faces won't recall who I
was
Maybe my firm has become an international combine, somebody else has
ordered that machine
Or maybe another firm ordered it and mine went bankrupt, maybe the
building itself has been levelled without a trace
I walk across the boulevard, here's the office, the doorman greets me
I go up to my room, my boss comes across the corridor, I clear my
throat to tell him
"I'm sorry, it wasn't my fault, actually I died a long time ago

That's why I couldn't come back right away, for two years I sat in
a wheelchair . . ."
But my boss smiles and passes on as if he hadn't even noticed my
absence, I step into my room
There sits my typewriter, my letter is in it, with an empty space
where there should be a word in the third line from the bottom
I had forgotten all about it and at five o'clock when I can go home,
I won't know where my home is
But now it's only three o'clock in the afternoon, I have plenty of
time so I will go out for fifteen minutes
And have some coffee, and I will come back and it will be easy to
find that right adjective

Translated from the Hungarian
by John Robert Colombo

THE MESSAGE

For Marshall McLuhan

The messenger arrived out of breath. The dancers stopped their pirouettes, the torches lighting the palace walls flickered for a moment, the hubbub at the banquet table died down, a roasted pig's knuckle froze in mid-air in a nobleman's fingers, a general behind the pillar stopped fingering the bosom of the maid of honour.

"Well, what is it, man?' asked the King, rising regally from his chair. "Where did you come from? Who sent you? What is the news?" Then after a moment, "Are you waiting for a reply? Speak up, man!"

Still gasping for breath, the messenger pulled himself together. He looked the King in the eye and said hoarsely: "Your Majesty, I am not waiting for a reply because there is no message because no one sent me. I just like running."

Translated from the Hungarian
by John Robert Colombo

STEPHAN G. STEPHANSSON

NOSTALGIA

If you come home during the spring,
when twilight lasts for hours
in a magic ring of glaciered mountains,

if you come home to this valley
where, as a boy, you fought for fun
and ran, almost as if you had somewhere to go,

then it will happen —
everything you were sure of once
and now know nothing of will seem
to haunt those moors and dells

and something of what you loved
and endured here will be reflected
in the dew, as you discover it
on swaths of hay, waking up again.

Translated from the Icelandic
by Michael Patrick O'Connor
and Thorvaldur Johnson

ELEGY

You are asleep now, Sigrid:
your closed eyes and locked lips
signal a peace which your cheeks
would deny in their deadly pallor.

As the dying day lights your tomb
and the freezing ocean guards it,
the surging wild Atlantic waves
have become your foster-sisters

Translated from the Icelandic
by Michael Patrick O'Connor
and Thorvaldur Johnson

ROBERT BRUNNER

THREE POEMS

The evening caught up with my journey,
I'm wading through a splashing blue
Above — there blink the stars like candles,
The pond is lit: there swims the moon.

I am engulfed in ringing silence,
I breathe the fragrance of the night.
Days-soldiers join me, always singing,
The marching songs make our steps light.

The dawn steals up through a sleeping forest
The night and I — we were alone.
She is a funny poetess
And always helps me with the rhyme.

* * *

It's an inexorable irony of fate:
The pleasant comes to us but for a moment.
You flashed across my sky, swift like a star
And then dissolved into a vision.

You're complex. Still, you're all simplicity,
Just like the Pythagorean solution.
But I am threatened from above by emptiness,
And from within — by indecision.

* * *

Like grimaces, like smiles
Senseless words are quivering
Whimsical and strange,
They gallop drunkenly

Without logic or meaning
They hang in the air.
The useless hours run away,
Hunchbacked, camel-like.
The night falls onto my shoulders,
The candles in the house went out.
And, melting into the darkness,
I am alone with myself.

Translated from the Russian
by E.Z.

J. I. SEGAL

AT MY WEDDING

At my wedding
a red-haired madman fiddled
on the smallest gentlest little fiddle;
he played his sweet lament
and fabled song
while other fiddlers watched in dumb amazement.

Where did he learn it,
this red-haired simpleton?
When you consider that he lived and worked
in backward villages,
and played only at drunken gentile brawls;
if you can picture it, he could hardly
scratch together a handful of holy words —
not even to save himself.
As for sleeping, he bedded on a wooden bench,
and if a servant
gave him radishes from the master's garden,
he was fed.

It was at my wedding this poor devil played,
no one could stand still, yet all were rooted,
ears in the air like pointed spears,
while the little fiddle tenderly caressed
and fiercely scored the people,
tore them to bits, flayed them and drew blood
to all their veins
until strung as taut as violin strings
the old folk, doddering, cried out for mercy.

Translated from the Yiddish
by Miriam Waddington

OLD MONTREAL

There's an old back street in Montreal
That was once the center of town,
Now the stone walls are yellow and burnt out,
And there's a broken-down church which God forsook

When he moved away to a new cathedral;
Yet whenever I walk that way
I imagine I hear ghostly bells ringing
Behind those ash-grey walls.

A little way down is an oblong cemetery
With small headstones, and smack in the middle
Stands a tall stained marble column
Keeping its long watch.

Not far away is the harbor market
With high buildings, wooden and blind,
And you can see a dirty red flag
Hung out for no reason at all, teasing the wind.

Between these narrow streets and glimpsing walls
The chimney of a dockside ship pokes out,
And a midday thread of smoke goes curling up
As from some cosy winter house.

Translated from the Yiddish
by Miriam Waddington

LATE AUTUMN IN MONTREAL

The worm goes back to the earth
the wind glitters and sharpens his sword;
where did all the colored leaves fly
to, anyway? The branches are all locked
in a vise of sleep; the skies aspire
to climb higher, their clear-blue
washes over the rooftops and stillness
assures us that all is well.
Our churchy city becomes even more pious
on Sundays, the golden crosses shine and gleam
while the big bells ring with loud
hallelujahs and the little bells answer
their low amens; the tidy peaceful streets
lie dreaming in broad daylight murmuring
endearments to me who am such a Yiddish Jew
that even in my footsteps they must hear
how the music of my Yiddish song sounds
through the rhythm of my Hebrew prayer.

Translated from the Yiddish
by Miriam Waddington

TEACHING YIDDISH

The children from my neighborhood
all come to me to learn Yiddish:
I tell them not to open their books,
I want to look at them and read
their faces as if they were pages
in a book; I want to know and be known,
so this is how I talk to them
without ever saying a word.

Dear boys and girls, Yiddish sons
and daughters, I want to teach you
what you've come to study but first
I have to learn how to read you I
have to write you and describe you
as you are and I don't really want
to be your teacher but an older
brother; so what shall we do?

First I think I'll read a story
by Sholem Aleichem just to see how much
you know about Yiddish laughter.
If you can laugh with real Yiddish flavor
at one of Sholem Aleichem's stories
I won't need further proof;
you'll do well with chumish in Yiddish
and even with gemorah in Yiddish,
and with literature naturally —
in what but Yiddish?

But you're laughing already
even before we get to Sholem Aleichem's
Motl Paisie the Cantor's son:
so today we're having our first lesson
in Yiddish laughter and all around me
shine your open faces and your lively eyes;
so let's tackle Sholem Aleichem head on
and go into a huddle of laughter.

Translated from the Yiddish
by Miriam Waddington

A JEW

My comrades are all such travellers
buzzing around in planes,
with one look they take the measure
of the wide bend of the sky.

If they have breakfast in Montreal
they drink coffee in New York,
of course that's all very grand,
even wonderful — but also queer.

Theirs are pleasures I renounce
especially on rainy days
when I can sit down beside the window
and think about an old wayside inn;

And how a cart full of Hasidim
drove up there late one night
and changed the simple little inn
to a beautiful palace;

And how the small band of faithful
sat around the wooden table
as radiant as if they were gathered
in the corridors of heaven.

Later I couldn't even remember
the Torahs and Haggadahs
but my heart is still full
of sweet worshipful longing.

It's no use my turning east
and it's no use my praying west,
I'm forever on the road, in transit,
dragging my baggage of exile.

That world is all gone now,
there's no monument to mark it,
and the only leaf left from the deluge
is a page in a Yiddish book.

So what is the leaf's green message
what stories does it bring?
only that a tree stood on the road
lighted by a single star.

The tree is still standing there
with the little star on its branch,
and it shines so strangely on the road
and the tree too has grown strange;

But it survives, my Jewish tree,
like a talisman of homecoming
and it longs to gather all us Jews
from our spaceless boundaries of loss.

Translated from the Yiddish
by Miriam Waddington

AUNT DVORAH

Our only aunt called Dvorah
Has gone and left us too,
And on her grave is carved a small Menorah
And on each side a slender stalk of wheat.

That is how the stonecutter Reb Nachem
Worked it out, and in between, her name;
We stand and gaze into religious silence
As from our lips there falls a last amen.

No member of her family survived her,
Her comely daughters, Esther and Hadassah,
Were lost in the great burning
Beyond the ghetto walls, in some side street.

And when they brought them home to her,
Their bodies raped and spoiled, well do I recall
How Dvorah clamped her mouth in iron silence
And sat, held in its bitter vise for days.

Widening her sorrow by their narrow graves
Our auntie used to sit, and in the evenings take
Her children's clothes and thoughtfully caress
Their measure; then shivering and bleak

She'd close the trunk and draw over her face
A darkness deeper than cavernous wastes
Of empty cupboards and more desolate
Than all those hangers peeled and bare.

Translated from the Yiddish
by Miriam Waddington

SCENARIO

The enemy returns
home to his German village,
and the white blossom on the tree
waves to him, bends to him,
smiles to him, "Welcome!"

His dog jumps up to meet him
and trembles with recognition,
and all around him lie his fields
as fresh and frank as summer.

In the doorway of his house
waits the housewife, pale and dear.
Lost in the joyous pulse of dream
she stands rooted and still as a bird.

He runs toward her
and she falls into his arms;
all is husband and wife between them,
together they enter their warm house.

But I, whom the German enemy destroyed
in seed and root, in branch and bud,
whose last living child he has killed,
and whose native city he has bent
from its ancient Polish pride —
I am the one who in my rags,
my ribbons, and my pure bright hate,
remain outside, and like a beaten cur
I must watch and see

How these German trees still celebrate
the summer's whiteness, and German fields

submit their earth to the sharpened plow,
while in the barn German horses

Bear German colts, silky and fair,
which German lads will mount and ride
possessing July and the burning sun
between fertile forests of wheat and rye.

And Jewish children? Sealed within winds
and their quenched ashes and desolate crumbs;
and only the emptiness of street
will remember and miss them, and only
the echoing cobblestones will weep.

I know they will not ever be transformed
to innocence, they will never be
angels astride on palominos
in a blossoming heaven; they will never be such
as tumble through fields and gamboling, shout,
"Welcome!" around the feet of God.

Translated from the Yiddish
by Miriam Waddington

HANNES OJA

STONES

Stones have endured.
We do not notice their change,
a grain of sand from a crumbled piece of granite.
A heavy, unchanging mass, gray-headed,
they bear the heaviness of days,
contemplate life without complaint, without lament.

Ridges, left by the Ice Age,
   look out across a flat clay ground
at gray houses of a village,
deep in the same stony peace.
Defiant, the ridges look at the village:
come, let us see who can endure longer.

Stones leave but a narrow passage
for the village street,
they form a hedge around the neck of fields,
a rosary from the days of serfdom,
a long stone chain that reaches
from village to village,
a thin mark of a meager field

and a meager fate.

Stones endure in their place,
roots deep in the soil,
even the moss spreads over them a green cover.
Children come skipping, jumping,
I'm the stone king!
You —
You are a stoneless orphan.

Translated from the Estonian
by the Author

THOUGHT WANTS TO KNOW

Thought surfaces as a fish
  for a moment above water,
and leaves a bursting bubble
glittering in rainbow colors,
leaves ripples that disappear in widening circles.

Thought seeks clarity,
seeks a way out of its own
  twilight and tangled thicket,
seeks light and truth.

Water moves heavy as tin,
underneath it shoals of paradoxes
whirl like banks of arrows.

Thought wants to know
what is behind thought.

Thought believes in the kinship
  of all thoughts,
believes that underbrush and thicket
  will give way to open spaces.

Thought believes that it is possible
to discover the countries behind thought
  by the light of the lamp of inspiration
  that penetrates darkness.

Translated from the Estonian
by the Author

LUIGI ROMEO

PENETANGUISHENE IN OCTOBER

(for G.M.)

The chlorophyll seeps by night
out of the Canadian maple
to fade away into the banks of the Huron.

Color screens
gradually faint on the road
amid the yellow and the dessicated blood,
awaiting the death of the brown.

The wild rice
still splashes in the water
watching the trees
stripped to shame,
and a leafy shroud is unwound
before the feet of Death.

Sky-blue, undines,
skipping,
doomed, run from the wind:
the cold clap breaks
from the North
in a sky where warmth has vanished.

Penetanguishene is already despairing
in the agonies of an obstinate struggle
with time.

Its final cries
tomorrow will assume a maw
of frozen snow
and a cradle, in the green of spring.

Translated from the Italian
by Rita Martin

ANDREAS SCHROEDER

THE EDGE

It was difficult to pour the steel. He persisted,
burning himself often; the steel became excited at
the smell of his flesh. Continually, it lashed about,
trying to harden into the form of a ring. But when
the glaciers moved over the hills into his window,
it was a knife, cooled, its perspiration dried.

He began to stroke it with files; he cut the days
from their months carefully, testing temper and
blade. Many hours lay strewn about his work bench
when it was done.

The crowd was huge, the roar continual, but when
he stepped onto the stage it seemed he had cut
the vocal cords of the crowd with the single up-
swing of his knife. Noise flittered away
confetti-like on a fading wind. Everyone waited
for the blacksmith's trick.

Suddenly, without warning, the knife began to sink,
its glittering eyes unaccountably malicious, and
the blacksmith's face turned grey with fear as he
fought to face what he had made — they struggled
without words in the silence of a crowded morning,
high above hands below.

Later, one said the knife had jumped into his heart.
Another claimed he had forced it in himself.

Translated from the German
by the Author

GREEN HEAVENS

A madness had been born, and the mill stood gaping
in the empty green heat. High above the sawdust burner
a pair of silent vultures stretched their net about the
sun. The sun seemed crying; now and then a white-hot
tear dripped into the aluminum-covered burner. Here and
there a chain creaked monotonously. It was during the
most unexplainable of times.

He was not taller than the mill entrance and was
therefore not obliged to stoop. He entered, and immediate-
ly the interior melted before his strength. Slowly he
advanced to the beginning of the mill life. And fell.
Tied with huge blue chains he passed through the saw
and was cut down through the middle. They pulled off
his skin and reduced him to a four-sided beam. The pro-
cedure was repeated and he fell apart into five fragments.
He rumbled down a chained embankment, was caught up and
neatly stacked in a pile.

In time he stood up and circled the mill again;
slowly, deliberately. Suddenly a noise like the gabbling
of geese reached him from a dark corner, and a huge Indian
stepped out into the sunlight. His upper front teeth
were missing and he wore grey tin plates in front of his
eyes. He blinked at the intruder through slits in the
plates. Then, "They haven't arrived yet," he said, tiredly,
without expression, rubbing his right boot against a shovel.
"They're still growing." "Oh," the other said, equally
expressionless. And then they both fell silent, ashamed.
It was a dying hope at best . . .

Translated from the German
by the Author

AN EXCHANGE

" . . . et pour s'etablir dans le monde, on fait tout ce qu'on peut pour y paraitre etabli . . . " There was a noise on the sidewalk beside the front lawn. The old man got up and crept to the window. The ancient cathedral clock, its gnawed stumps of hands badly behind the times but still creeping, trembled at three o'clock, morning. The two faces, from sidewalk and window, met in a neon flash, then quickly dissolved. Fog swirled about the street light on the corner; only two eyes glowed against the barred window. There was the sound of shuffling footsteps. The man on the sidewalk was coming back, slowly, dragging a piece of lead on a rope behind him. The two eyes followed him carefully; his long skirt, his wide floral hat and the perambulator he was pushing before him. There was a large dog in the buggy, sleeping. The man jerked along, sending the perambulator on ahead with an occasional kick, but the dog didn't wake up. He may have been dead. The lump of lead rumbled along behind the night walker, dragging bits of leaves, an old piece of newspaper. The blakies on the man's shoes rang out his progress. Kick, click, rumble. Kick, click, rumble. Two greyish-yellow eyes at the attic window. The sounds faded out into the fog. Two ears appeared at the window. Kick, click, rumble. Softly. It was gone. The old man crept back to his book. " . . . et le soleil ni la mort ne se peuvent regarder fixement . . . "

Translated from the German
by the Author

WACLAW IWANIUK

WHO CALLS WHAT A POEM

Yes, the poet does
what he can —
collects strips of
words, chips of sounds
links them together
with an invisible thread
like a spider
moistening sore
nerves and gathering
in striae his
own darkness, and at
every turn erects
signes made of
his private passions
similar to Homer's
marble voices; but
others wonder
see there perhaps
Chagall's flying scene
where the black
dense beard hunts
the heavy barricades
of clouds; where the white
goat in pink woolens
grazes in green air;
Yes, the poet does
what he can —
they regard him
as a charlatan, not even
an alchemist deforms
words, extracts them

from the gum of rules and codes,
violating the sanctity of grammar,
to emerge at last
with something
so painfully mutilated
what he then calls
a POEM.

Translated from the Polish
by the Author

APRES LE DELUGE

In our world even the innocent birds
Are swept from their nests by the raging storm;
Turning towards the sky a harmless dove
Will soon become a ruse of propaganda.
The artist sells his soul for any slogan
And art is measured by the empty word.
Time drops towards darkness
The moon escapes earth's apparition
Dreaming of Ararat
We wait for the dove to bring to us
Swiftly the laurel leaf.

What is salvation if those who survive
Hurry to be devoured again by night.
Bathed in the rising dawn, impatiently
We wait for the approaching night.
Our garden lies untended
The canary sleeps
And our lips cannot utter a word.
With a sack on our backs, and not salvation,
We carry with us our cemeteries.
Preferring chaos, though order is better
Preferring hell, though heaven is nearer
We measure God again with silver pieces
And christianity with cybernetics.
Temple in our time does not mean temple
Nor Bible — Bible.

Translated from the Polish
by Gustaw Linke

I FEAR CONTINUALLY THAT THE PREMATURE NIGHT

I fear continually that the premature night
Will hunt me down darkly one noon,
That time will betray me and I'll fall
And with lips attuned to earth
I shall drink as though I had never known
The pit of isolation.
Surrounded by the unremembered calm
Of gentle hills and patient vegetation
I shall forget the horror of the earth.
Softly the whisper of abundant rose
Blooming like starfish
Will mingle with my flesh.
The melancholy pines
Coerce the landscape. The heat-distorted trees —
Flat and dark physiognomy —
Are wrapped in the quiet of oxygenized hills.

And all around the summer column burns
While the night collapses, expiating.

Who does not love this architecture
Who has not loved to climb the airy stairs
Refreshed by daily tidal foam?
Is it not better to hide within the calm
And to take cover under stone, to cry with marble's cry,
To see the moths like angels raging in the ruins
And like the saints to despair with blinded hands?
To disbelieve the heaven's iron fires
Although it tempts with flowers, and underpinned with fog,
Sweats with dew.
Poets like pilgrims flock, although they know
They've been betrayed again. Virtue is feared.

Thin air breaks under the word
Stony waves scatter the sand
The vineyard rushed down into the bay
Nothing remains after a burned-out day
Except the ruins spoken of in song
Which the poets have renamed: defeat
The poem like a supplicant kneels down
Does not reveal, though it will try to soothe
And even if like a hermit it believes
It will be here forever out of place.

Translated from the Polish
by Gustaw Linke

ALL THAT IS MINE

All that is mine
the earth took —
the Punic boats, the Vistula sand
the bridge strung across like a white dove —
all that is mine
was burned
broken
silenced —

The Kingdom of smoke
the Vistula ashes
the Vistula sands —
the doves had their wings broken
the bridges — their ribs
the people — their eyes.

Only water is deeper than life
it collects, carries beyond horizons
  the wings
the ribs
the sheaves of eyelids
all the Vistula harvest —
it collects and carries them beyond the horizons.

All that is mine —
the wings
the ribs
the eyesight harvest
await in my harbor
awakening.

Translated from the Polish
by Z. Folejewski

EPILOGUE

Returning home, I will enter the room
across the empty threshold, the door and dead walls.
Finding the waxy stigma, and a spider's loom
weaving its deadly net. The window's ghostly holes.

Here mother sat. The table is not there,
instead of the bench the shadow on the floor.
As if they dragged her body by her white hair,
and let the oven swallow her. Ashes and night.

On the other side in the faded wood
sat father in a chair bent with old-age pain,
holding the Bible in his hands,
with face turned up, reading from mother's eyes.

The chair is gone, turned easily into ashes
The content of the word was tested by fire.
When Father tried to defend my Mother
His head was smashed by a rifle butt.

Translated from the Polish
by Z. Folejewski

EINAR PALL JONSSON

THE LAUNDRESS

She worked as a housemaid, then as a laundress
in small town Winnipeg, full of emigres speaking
every language except her own: she was Icelandic
and as she worked she sang the old Icelandic hymns
and songs: the songs had all her joy, they brought
all her peace. She kept reaching for the language
that got lost in her life. She could never speak it
again, though it always measured her breath.

Late one summer, as she lay dying, she sang again
the Icelandic hymns, sang in her mother tongue,
an other tongue for us; and as we lay her
in a foreign grave, we, who know no Icelandic,
who know then almost nothing of what she loved
and lived by, say our prayers over her in English.

Translated from the Icelandic
by Michael Patrick O'Connor
and Thorvaldur Johnson

PAVEL JAVOR

THE AUTUMN

I

On the autumn woods the heavy rains
are settling —
The white, slim grace
of your warmth still lingers on
in the ring's etched trace.

On the autumn woods the gunfire drifts
as the rifle sighs —
By the morning light the pillow hid,
your weeping eyes . . .

On the autumn woods the heavy rains
are sounding, sounding . . .
I cannot sleep, I hear the hoofs
of black horses pounding . . .

A voice calls out to us:
My love, I cannot stay.
Stronger than love the voice calling away.

II

The lonely moon above us
— a bright coin on display —
A shadow of helpless anguish,
sweeping your voice away —

A few more autumns passing
and then we shall be gone.
And still the corn will rustle,
the birds fly on . . .

Translated from the Czech
by Alfred French

FAR FROM YOU

A young breeze trips across the grass,
The river flows without return.
Our hearts in pangs, alas,
Feel far-off throes that wound and burn.

You await me in the house alone,
Your dog still watches on the stair.
The gulf of distance makes me moan,
and longing that I cannot bear.

The same sun gives your mouth its kiss,
The same wind soothes your lips with dew,
The same moon peers at you with bliss,
But I am now no longer I
And you, perhaps, no longer you.

Time and the river flow for ever,
Time and the river wait for no man,
Time, yes, and love, flow thus for me —
Kisses and young fidelity
And longing for a far-off woman . . .

Translated from the Czech
by Watson Kirkconnell

SILENCE FALLS . . .

Steps have faded: silence falls
Upon the muted scene.
Drowsing like the pallid moon
Along a winter stream —

Lost, I blunder, young in grief,
And know all poems lied.
Relic of a vanished past,
Whose echo died . . .

Translated from the Czech
by Alfred French

THE TORPOR

As in the muffled depths of a well
we stand here isolated —
Through the piercing, icy silence,
there comes no sound.
Too late now to fret
and call ourselves the ill-fated,
when the anchor of home
can find no ground.

So, one by one,
past the brink we fall
like a stone to the depths,
and, like hope, are gone —
and the wound does not bleed
or hurt now at all.
And nothing is done,
nothing done . . .

Translated from the Czech
by Alfred French

THE EXILE

The day I went away,
"How soon will you come back?"
enquired my little son.
The flowers have left the trees
and now the corn is in
and the leaves are gone . . .

The nights are creeping on
and the time is never here.
The cold comes drearily.
I stretch my puny arms
but what can they avail,
and who will comfort me?

To the bottom of the well
has fluttered from the tree
the ruddy maple leaf.
Oh, God, when shall I calm
a heart that endlessly
is tight with grief?

Translated from the Czech
by Alfred French

ALL OF YOU

Cottage behind the village,
With the whip-sticks of high poplars to guard you,
With the yellow outcry of marsh marigolds,
On the dyke warmed by the sun!

And my mother, dainty, red from the oven,
With a fan of wrinkles round her mild eyes,
And my old father, astraddle in the fields,
Gigantic and good . . .

Trees, bridesmaids with blossoming cherries,
Skirts bunched up,
Shoots of potatoes, yellow, peeping out of furrows,
The sad singing of a finch, languishing in dry branches —

How remote it all is, how futile!

From the depths of the valleys
Toward the stars
The odour of honeycombs of ploughed earth,
Black and warm like the bellies of mares.
An ocean of corn ripples with a mysterious song,
Poor stubble-fields whose wounded stalks
Spout drips on bare legs —

The smoke of autumn fires
Advancing along the valleys like a hooded army,
Snow butterflies, which we caught in our hot palms,
That settled on our eyes, eyelashes, curls of hair —
How remote it all is, how sad!

All my kin,
Driven out into the world, out of the stillness of cornfields,
Who waste away in a blight of nostalgia,
And you, there, strangers in your own country,
All of you whom I love with a bitter love . . .
As of smothered fires, dying toward the morning,
To the high stars smoulders my song

Translated from the Czech
by Bennie Thomson

REINHARD

WINTER'S FIELDS

winter's fields
fell between us
and levelled hills:

there is nothing between us.
cold crept inside you
a flower
tired of the sun
tired of gestures mimicking
the sun. leaves shield
your face
downcast and
leaves shield

your face and
iceflowers
blossom on your panes.

soon your ink
fades into the yellowing page
of your letter and
all your feelings
have come to be words.

Translated from the German
by the Author

NOBODY KNOWS

heavy the fog settles
on the sea. no groaning.
quite mute
hardly perceptible
it spreads.

what can i learn from that?
nobody knows,
and so i turn
within me. What do i
find there? only an image

of myself: between
my legs my hand clasps
a pen.
also
in the labyrinth of scattered papers
an empty inkwell hits my eye.

what can i learn from that?
nobody knows,
and so i slip
into the pen's interior.
there no ink blackens.
there acts the pressure of my hand.

Translated from the German
by the Author

I LOOK OUTSIDE

i look outside:
on ground
of the hand's
presence.
nobody knows. and i
dissolve. nobody knows.

*Translated from the German
by the Author*

SIGNS

your frequency shows
on one end
of the scale,
a shudder on the other.
sometimes i receive you
from very distant places,
and you send images to me:
you, curled around
your curled up cat;
a crow,
a black caw
above the white prairie.
and when you don't get through
i shudder.

Translated from the German
by the Author

ANDRZEJ BUSZA

SMALL APOCALYPSE

there behind the trees
a black mountain
awaits us all

it is nothing
a gap in the blue
at night
a hole in the sky

hunched
formless as asphalt
it creeps hissing
through the spruce trees
towards our valleys

where white sheep
and rabbits with transparent ears
nibble the grass

we leave our ploughs
and spinning wheels
and casting a final glance
at our farmsteads
we briefly
take stock of our conscience

from the mosaic landscape
a dog barks
cave canem

it is good that the mountain moved
on a week day

Translated from the Polish
by Jagna Boraks and
Michael Bullock

TIGER

my tiger
calls to me
through the fog

golden
in a cage of purple stripes
he burns
through the embers of his pupils

thrice foolish
like the *Bandar-log*
I cover my eyes
my ears and mouth

and wait
in the blazing crown
of dying trees

when the sour breath
licks the boles
my heart
claws at the bars of my ribs

Translated from the Polish
by Jagna Boraks and
Michael Bullock

WOMAN WITH CELLO AND FOXES

at the crossroads
a woman stands transfixed

waiting
for the apple tree
to blossom again

she presses a black cello
to her thigh

and trembles as the chords
swarm through her flesh like ants

three foxes
each of a different autumn colour

scent blood
on the strings of the wind

Translated from the Polish
by Jagna Boraks and
Michael Bullock

ASTROLOGER IN THE UNDERGROUND

with an indifferent rumble
a train
vanished
into the tunnel

on the deserted platform
a gray-bearded magus
calculates
the malignant conjunction
of Mars
and stern Venus

what does he care
about my girl
transformed into a celadon song
her breasts overgrown with bark
a trickle of sunlight
on her silver-birch thigh

Translated from the Polish
by Jagna Boraks and
Michael Bullock

THE POND

a sheet of light
divides it from the sky

above
race the sky-blue peacocks of the wind

the pines
explode again and again
with sunfire

inside
among the roots of darkness
circle time-fish
set for midnight

it is a dangerous pond

it lies in wait
like a mirror

Translated from the Polish
by Jagna Boraks and
Michael Bullock

OPERATION

he was placed
in the clamp of silence

above him
the ceiling of the sky
below
the sheet of still waters

slowly
bolts were tightened

he hung
in the void
gasping
till he could breathe no more

with an involuntary spasm
he set the cogs in motion
the electronic gears moved
crushing the brittle bubble of his heart

then the grooves and sockets were re-oiled

Translated from the Polish
by Jagna Boraks and
Michael Bullock

FIRE

only with fire
can you quench fire

fire drives out fire
as iron drives out iron

in the black scabbard of smoke
the core of the blaze hisses

like a white-hot wire
burning the hands

you cannot stanch the veins of night
with your fingers

you cannot check the light
when it bleeds from the body

only fire
can turn back the cortege of darkness

only fire
burns fire

Translated from the Polish
by Jagna Boraks and
Michael Bullock

NIGHT

at the top
of the black house
a child
wrestles with dreams

above the clear brow
darkness
alive with croaking beaks
spreads its huge horns

the sea-wind
churning sand and foam
shakes the slate roof
as if to uproot it

the vortex of the zodiac
slowly draws
obdurate stones
into the deeps of the sky

where one-eyed nebulae shine
and the Cloud of Magellan
spawns contagion

wombed by walls
we burn horoscopes
paper blackens in mourning
hands fall to the ground
like empty nests

Translated from the Polish
by Jagna Boraks and
Michael Bullock

ATOLL

dread was daybreak
on the black bough of the sea
the moon raged
like a gong
struck by lightning

thunderbolt after thunderbolt
rolled
along the corrugated waves
and night sank
in chasms of foam

we entered the harbour

the bay
in silent mourning
welcomes us
with the claws of volcanic rocks

the small rusty steamer
sways
in the island's single eye
like a splinter
upon the dark glazed surface of a well

the pilot
on the bridge
surrounded by a flock
of glassy-eyed sheep
takes a briar pipe
not a flute
from his lips

saying
anchors are useless here
the sea is bottomless

Translated from the Polish
by Jagna Boraks and
Michael Bullock

ART

behold an incomplete tree
a black fork
with a place for the moon

this sight yearns
it is unconsummated
like a celadon vase
without asters

the lunatic the lover and the poet
bend the sky
to fullness
in underwater dreams

caressing out of twilight
a pearl
the moon

Translated from the Polish
by Jagna Boraks and
Michael Bullock

BLACK

black
the swans glide
nailed to their shadows
storm-black sails
edged with sunlight

hands
which once
hollowed out bark
wither
like bindweed
on a bleached wall

through fingers
seep
golden rust
and the swan
rising
into darkness

Translated from the Polish
by Jagna Boraks and
Michael Bullock

ARVED VIIRLAID

FROSTED MIRROR 1

Wars have been fought before
in front of a frosted mirror
an answer has been dug from your own face
hand on the sleigh's runner

A scream has been heard before
from within the frosted mirror
there was a sickly browling
a finger was caught in the frozen runner's grip

An answer has been given before
the frosted mirror like a drink
warmed the belly like champagne
the heart's finger in ice

Wars have been fought within oneself before
wars and fingers have been chopped
the heart framing the mirror
oh speck!

The frozen runner for a ring round the finger
is a wedding before the frosted mirror
a paw in the clutch of Death

Translated from the Estonian
by Taimi Ene Moks

FROSTED MIRROR 2

Breath warms the mirror glass
warms it to change it back
the play of icy gusts
scorches the heart

A fire has scorched
the pollen and melting sand
the fire has hardened
sky and water into an ice field

He speaks who talks buried in sand
the finger warmed the window's ice
just as yesterday it warmed the ice
you will remain without the mirror's warmth

Blood of the heart's juice has dripped
dripped from a lifeless sponge
he who let the last drop fall
has taken the flame from the hearth

The ice is warmed by breath
it warms the ice for a long time
the mirror doesn't see in the dark it doesn't see
the struggle of shadows in ice

Translated from the Estonian
by Taimi Ene Moks

FROSTED MIRROR 3

The light of daisies
rocked the evening's pain to sleep
in the nest of the flames of dawn
the moon slept hurrah because
she slept with snow fur around her feet

Amid the daisies' light
the dawn pinched the birds tweet tweet
and hoohoo and hoohoo
the ringed hand of the snowstorm
struck the fur on the wolves' backs

Daisies adorned the nest
when bare branches were left
and three drops of blood in ice
bleached in the sun's light

The red drops bleached a long time
into the face of the ice to the last drop
therefore the acid of pain
grows into the flesh with the ice

Translated from the Estonian
by Taimi Ene Moks

READER III: And so what if poetry
is the thread in the needle's eye,
stitching the patterns of a dhroud
into the bridal gown.

And so what

Even towards silence all roads run
with the happy yapping of puppies.

Trickles and worms
knot the fringes of the garment,
and the Bride's arms
are always open for embraces,

for thought carries fire into the earth —
roots full of dynamite.
With every heartbeat the earth
pumps fire
to sleep in granite.

Translated from the Estonian
by Astrid Ivask

GOD SAID

God said to me:
"Look,
I promise you anything
as long as you dare
look me in the face!"

I listened to his words.
I trembled.
I dared not
raise my eyes.

But later,
when He called me,
I raised my laughing face:
my fear was gone.

And a time came
when God no longer dared
look me in the face

Translated from the Estonian
by Taimi Ene Moks

WHERE CAN YOU GO ANY MORE?

Trees bow down to the ground
in fog and autumn.
Along the ground whirl
fallen leaves
and black field rats.

Over the empty sea
walk the angry storms
toward the fishermen's sleeping huts.
And then — the sky begins to fall.

But on the doorstep stands a girl.
Her long cool fingers
she presses against her breast:
to go or to stay?

On the doorstep stands a girl.
Icy winds whip her face.
In her eyes trembles
a restless light
and her fingers stir:
to go or to stay?

But the rats are leaping
merrily and roguishly
over the torsos of the trees.
And, look, into one stump
a heavy, bloody axe is struck!

Where can you go any more?

Translated from the Estonian
by Taimi Ene Moks

EXILE

I take my woman and go
over stone rivers
and salt deserts
to a distant land.

I light a fire
in a black rockpit.
I hunt in the sun,
which is blood-red
but colder than the moon.

And then, when the gray birds
circle in the air
and the ice crackles in crevices,
my descendants are born.

And then, when I am old
gray and shrivelled — a dwarf
in my dark cave,
my proud sons go forth.
They return to the land
which God has hidden from me.

And look,
they dig up
the sun buried in the marshes!
The stones sing in their hands
and fortresses rise
shining at the morning.

Translated from the Estonian
by Taimi Ene Moks

WANDERING AND FLEEING

Wander and flee
you must, son of man.

With insolence you are smitten
like wilted grass.
Grief devours you
like swarms of locusts
and you own no cave
where you can hide from yourself.

Son of man, where do you get the tenacity
to shout into the storm?
Where do you get the strength
to rise from your agony?

Stop, you fool,
before it's too late!

A voice echoes
from lands beyond graves:
"Die and be humble!"

But you die,
living curses on your lips.
You die making a fist:
your cooling fingers
trying to protect
a withered blossom.

Translated from the Estonian
by Taimi Ene Moks

RAMON MANSOOR

YESTERDAY

Yesterday: books
stuck to the air;
words, hot,
steamed from ashtrays;
looks lived in
by people:
Time was a man.

Yesterday: 2 eyes
and a child,
they searched for the night;
thoughts sought refuge
in self-love;
the sun slept
in the mouth of a man
old and dead;
Time lamented.

Translated from the Spanish
by the Author

REMEMBER

"And who shall teach an odour
back into the hearts of flowers."
L.F.M.

I remember you in the butterfly that dances on the leaf of mist and dies in the child's heart.

Smiling you said: "We are time, you and I," and you began to rain, and your rain was the first steps of words I listened to as they flowed away.

I remember you in the mirrored multitudes of two fingers pressed together, anxiously.

Translated from the Spanish
by the Author

YAR SLAVUTYCH

YOUR EYES

Your eyes reflected the warm sky
the daring of a lust
hiding out at night disguised as love

I didn't know who could judge
Eve's temptation
but I understood the temptation itself
that moment in August
when apple trees are all their own
and apples are ripe

The veto God felt obliged to pass
knocked the tops off a few mountains

and Adam's insatiable passion
reached the most distant stars

Translated from the Ukrainian
by the Author and M. P. O'Connor

SAP SWELLS IN THE BELLY OF MEMORY

I'd rather rot in soggy ground
running to a maple's roots
then at least there would be the colors
green leaves moving through

the blue sky   Then at least
the hardness of the vault or the justice
of God would know I never left
I died   The invaders killed me.

But I stayed all the same sharing
all the hardships caused by the shift
into the wrong season parcelling out
everything the new regime demanded

Sap swells in the belly of memory
I can see the Ukraine, greening through spring
I am floating over the maple trees
and I am nourishing them as much as I can

Translated from the Ukrainian
by the Author and M. P. O'Connor

THE HOUSE

VOICE II: On a summit ascending the banks of the Dnieper's
Far reaching blue
Where the ripening wheat in the sun's heat breaks foam
A house once stood. Immeasurably blessed, its
sovereign circle grew
Like the white crown of a poppy in the poplared wood.

The sea-foaming sound of the rain swells the river's
High rising banks.
The field with its huge yield of bread, grows, swells
Momentously. Abundant in their praise, man, woman,
swell with thanks
Boasting the good seed of a fruitful family.

Who came then? Who came by the soft stealth of midnight
To trouble the dust
Of the ancient ones? Daughters and sons: for the evil
of others
Who shall atone? In exile enduring, the blameless, the
innocent must,
Until their waiting wanes the spirit and the bone.

Without touch or direction the children of exile
Blindly go,
Redeeming the past, they re-live the last measure of home
Brimming memory and sight. Do they labor the truth,
seeking causes or knowing it so
Make real the dream prophetic as their fathers might?

From a summit descending smoke ruins, black fires
That rent the sky
Sounds and voices in one chanting unison, shiver the house
Like a prayer. The dried poplars crackle. The silence
snaps, barren and dry,
And the wind thins in a wolf-howl, holding nothing there.

Translated from the Ukrainian
by Myra Haas

EPILOGUE

(Dedicated to the two hundred Ukrainian authors killed in the 1930's during the reign of Stalin)

No wreaths were plaited to your name,
No trumpets heralded your dying.
Your wives and children never came
To bless the ground where you are lying.

Perhaps your noble bones decay
Ignored in some Siberian woodland.
Perhaps your ashes blew away
And circle up above our good land.

Who knows? Perhaps your stalwart soul
Stood firm, rebuking the assassin.
Perhaps it fell before the goal,
Accursed, inworthy of its passion.

O God, show mercy to them all,
To them who broke, whose tongues betrayed them,
And prayed to Satan at the wall,
To those Red devils who dismayed them.

And with eternal peace repay
The tortured martyrs of the basement
Who walked as on a holiday
Against the promise of effacement,

Who faced the bullets with disdain
And turned their killers' pride to water
Outlasting every thrust of pain
And proving prouder at the slaughter.

Bless those who made each hope sublime
And wrought from truth a thing of beauty
To bridge the abysses of time
And span the spheres of life and duty.

Commanders of the souls of men,
The future will attend your bother
When sons are welcomed home again,
Each one the gladness of his father.

And brothers, sisters will rejoice
When men are men once more, not chattel!
Then people will exalt the voice
Which marshalled them in battle.

Translated from the Ukrainian
by the Author

THE DAYS ARE SHORT

The days are short, the nights are shorter still,
Above me Heaven's half-sphere shrinks to pond size.
How will I satisfy my heart-born will
With even endless space wherein this world lies?

The roads extend, the rivers bend and flow,
The mountains mutely contemplate the luster!
Time's witcher, Man, deciphers Heaven's glow,
Unriddles stars from their disturbing cluster.

Translated from the Ukrainian
by the Author

TAKEO NAKANO

MY HANDS

My hands tremble
As I sign my naturalization papers
Making me a Canadian citizen
And Canada my final resting place.

Translated from the Japanese
by Robert Y. Kadoguchi

CONTRIBUTORS

T. HIRAMATUS is widely known among Japanese and Japanese Canadians for his Haiku and Waka. *The Fish* was selected from some fifteen thousand entries to be read before Emperor Hirohito. Mr. Hiramatus lives in Toronto.

ROBERT Y. KADOGUCHI is very active among Japanese cultural groups in Toronto. He translated both the Hiramatus and Nakano selections in this volume.

Presently GEORGE FALUDY is a lecturer at Columbia University in New York. He is regarded by many as the greatest living poet writing in the Hungarian language, even though readers in Hungary have not been permitted to read his books since 1939. Faludy escaped the Nazi invasion and after moving through France and Morocco, he moved to the U.S.A. on President Roosevelt's invitation. He returned to Hungary after the war, but was figuratively interred at the infamous concentration camp in Recsk, after the Communist takeover in 1948. He finally escaped Hungary for the second time in 1956. For the past 13 years Faludy has been living in London, Malta, Toronto and New York. His work published in English includes *My Happy Days in Hell*, *Karoton* and he's recently completed a biography of Erasmus of Rotterdam.

GEORGE JONAS was born in Budapest, Hungary, and has been living in Canada since 1956. He is a television producer for the C.B.C. in Toronto. Two of his collections of poetry have been published to date (both by House of Anansi): *The Absolute Smile* and *The Happy Hungry Man*; his work has appeared in numerous English-language and Hungarian periodicals and anthologies. Presently he is at work on a novel.

HENRIKAS NAGYS was born in 1920 in Mazeikiai, Lithuania. He began his studies in architecture in 1940 but switched (1941-1943) to Lithuanian and German Literature at the University of Vytautas the Great in Kaunas. After fleeing Lithuania near the end of the war, he studied from 1945 to 1949 at the University of Innsbruck in Austria, majoring in German Literature and Art History. He earned his doctorate for a study of the work of Georg Trakl. He has taught at the Applied Art Institute in Freiburg and at the University of Montreal. He immigrated to Canada in 1951. Nagys' first poems appeared in Lithuania in 1938. Since then four books have been published. He has translated German, Canadian, and Latvian works into his native tongue. During the formative years of his writing he was part of the Zeme (Earth) movement of young Lithuanian writers and was one of the initiators and editors of the important journal *Literaturos Lankai* (now defunct). Since he came to Montreal, he has worked as a commercial artist, teacher, and editor of an emigre newspaper.

ALDONA PAGE was born in Lithuania and graduated from Wayne State University, Detroit. ROBERT PAGE is also a Wayne State graduate. Presently he teaches English at Temple University in Philadelphia. The Pages have translated poems by Nagys, a play by Antanas Skema, and a book by Julius Kaupas. Their work has appeared in *The Hudson Review, December, Lithuanus, The Literary Review, Canadian Review, Canadian Literature* and *Prism International.*

TULIN ERBAS lives in Sarnia, Ontario with her husband and two sons. Since 1966 she has been Canadian correspondent for the

Turkish newspaper, *Hurriyet*. Her first book, *Winds from Canada* was published in Turkey in 1970. She is now writing her second, *From Huron to Bosphorus.*

DR. NICHOLAS CATANOY was born in Rumania where he studied philosophy and medicine. Aside from being a physician, he is a research editor, literary critic, translator and lecturer in comparative Literature. He has written several books of poetry and art criticism. He immigrated to Canada in 1962. Presently he is a member of the society of Rumanian Writers in Exile (Rome), a contributor to *Books Abroad* (U.S.A.) and to *Poesie Vivante* (Switzerland), research editor for Gallimard (Paris), and consulting editor for Guadarrama (Madrid). He is editor of *Anthology of Rumanian Contemporary Poetry* (Penguin). Canadian debut: *Hic Et Nunc* (1968). *Flux Alb* (Rumanian and French poems, 1970). To be published in 1971: *Circumstante* (Rumanian Poems), 1972: *Journal Walpurgique* (novel).

BOGDAN CZAYKOWSKI is a member of the faculty of Slavonic Studies at the University of British Columbia. As well as being a poet, he has written and lectured widely about modern Polish and Canadian literatures. He has translated a volume of modern Canadian literature into Polish. Recently he has returned from a leave of absence in Europe where he was at work on a book about modern Polish poetry.

MICHAEL BULLOCK is a poet, playwright, fiction-writer and translator. He is the author of five volumes of poetry, two plays and two collections of short fictions, *Sixteen Stories As They Happened*, and *Green Beginning, Black Ending* (both published by The Sono Nis Press). He has translated well over a hundred full-length books and plays from German, French, and Italian, including three novels and seven plays by Max Frisch, four volumes of poems, numerous novels and several works on philosophy and aesthetics by such authors as Karl Jaspers, Martin Buber and Wilhelm Worringer. In 1966 he won the Schlegel-Tieck German Translation Prize presented by the Government of the German Federal Republic in conjunction with the British and German Publishers Associations.

CATHERINE LEACH teaches in the Slavonic Studies Department at the University of British Columbia. Formerly she taught at Berkeley where she translated much of the work of the Polish American poet, Czeslaw Milosz.

JOSE EMILIO PACHECO was born in Mexico City in 1939. He studied for several years at the National University of Mexico. He has translated numerous French and English-language poets into Spanish and contributed to Spanish-language journals including *Universidad de Mexico*, *Estaciones*, and the supplement, *Mexico en la Cultura*, in *Novedades*. A large selection of Pacheco's work appeared in the 1960 Aguilar anthology, *Anthologia de la Poesia Mexicana.* He has published six volumes including two volumes of short stories (*La Sangre de Medusa* and *El Viento Distante*), a novel (*Moriras Lejos*), and three volumes of poetry, *Los Elementos de la Noche* (1963), *Reposo Del Fuego* (1966) and *No Me Preguntes Como Pasa El Tiempo* (1969). The last volume received the 1969 Premio Nacional de Poesia Award. He has also edited several anthologies of Mexican writing. He has been in residence at the University of British Columbia for the past two years.

GEORGE MCWHIRTER's first book, *Catalan Poems*, was published in 1971 by Oberon. Born in Ireland, his poems, fictions, and translations have appeared widely in the English-speaking world. He is Associate Editor of *Contemporary Poetry of British Columbia.*

WALTER BAUER was born in Germany in 1904 and immigrated to Canada in 1952. He is the author of novels, novellas, essay and short story collections, plays, books for children and biographies, including a study of Nansen for which he received the first Albert Schweitzer Prize. Presently he teaches German at the University of Toronto.

HENRY BEISSEL was the controversial editor of the controversial (and now defunct) *Edge* magazine (not to be confused by the New Zealand magazine by that name). He is author of *New Wings for Icarus* (Coach House), a collection of poems, and he has just returned from Europe where he has been working on a novel and a collection of translations from the work of Peter Huchel.

GUTTORMUR J. GUTTORMSSON had the distinction of being the only significant writer in Icelandic on this continent who was born here. He was a close friend of fellow poet-farmer, Stephan G. Stephansson (whose work is also included in this volume.)

THORVALDUR JOHNSON is a former head of the Federal Research Centre, University of Manitoba, Winnipeg. A great champion of Icelandic Canadian culture.

SAMAR ATTAR was born in Damascus, Syria, where she received her "Licence en Lettres" in English Literature and in Arabic Literature. She came to Canada in 1965 and took her M.A. at Dalhousie University. She is now working on her Ph.D. at the State University of New York in Comparative Literature. She has published several poems, articles and short stories in Lebanese, Syrian and English-Language periodicals and newspapers. Presently she is preparing her critical study *The Influence of T. S. Eliot on Salah Abdel Sabour* for publication in the U.S.A.

GWENDOLYN MACEWEN is well-known to Canadians as poet, novelist, and translator. She won the Governor-General's Award for poetry in 1969. Her researches into Arabic cultures and heliolatry are extensive.

MANUEL BETANZOS-SANTOS is a member of the Executive of the League of Canadian Poets. He was born in Galicia, Spain in 1933 and is a graduate of the University of Madrid. He came to Canada in 1959 and has been teaching Spanish at McGill University since 1963. Six books of his poetry have been published (one selection in French, published in France) the most recent of which is *Cancion del Nino en la Ventana* (*Song of the Child at the Window*) (New York, 1970). Mr. Betanzos-Santos is editor-publisher of the little magazine *Boreal-Poesia Espanola en la Canada* and is a member of the Honorary Committee of the International Circle of Poets of Latin America.

RACHEL KORN's poems have been previously published in a series of programs produced for C.B.C.'s *Anthology* by John Reeves.

MIRIAM WADDINGTON teaches at York University. Her collection of poems, *Say Yes*, was published by Oxford University Press in 1969.

ROBERT ZEND was born in Budapest and there worked in film and as a freelance journalist and translator. He took his B.A. from the Peter Pazmany Science University in 1953. He left in 1956 to come to Toronto where, in 1958, he joined the C.B.C. as film librarian and then editor. In 1969 he received his M.A. from the University of Toronto, a grant from the Canadian Film Development Corporation to produce a film, and a scholarship from the Italian government to study in Italy. Many of his poems and articles have been published in Hungary and Canada.

JOHN ROBERT COLOMBO is the author of seven books of poetry and the editor of three, most recently *Neo Poems*, *How Do I Love Thee*, and *The Great San Francisco Earthquake and Fire*. He is the only living Canadian poet to have a volume of poetry translated into French: *La Grande Muraille de Chine*, translated by Jacques Godbout. His translations from the French appear in John Glassco's *The Poetry of*

French Canada in Translation. He is now finishing a book called *Translations from the English* which is not a book of translations at all but a collection of "found poems."

STEPHAN G. STEPHANSSON is among the most popular of the Canadian writers in Icelandic. His work has appeared previously in *Canadian Folklore* and on the "unofficial language" poetry series produced for C.B.C.'s *Anthology* by Mr. John Reeves.

MICHAEL PATRICK O'CONNOR is a graduate of Notre Dame University (U.S.A.) where he edited *The Juggler.* His translations and poetry have appeared in *Contemporary Literature in Translation, Prism International,* and numerous other English-language literary journals. He is presently a graduate student at the University of British Columbia.

ROBERT BRUNNER was born in Russia in Ekaterinoslaww. He is a physician. Previously his poems have appeared in the newspaper, *Russian Life,* in San Francisco and in *La Renaissance* in Paris.

J. I. SEGAL was a major North American writer in Yiddish. His work has appeared previously in English on C.B.C.'s *Anthology* and in *Canadian Literature.*

HANNES OJA is a factory worker in Toronto. He was born in 1919 in Martna, Estonia, and educated in Haapsalu secondary school and Uuemõisa Agricultural College. He served in both the Estonian and Finnish armies. In 1943 he escaped to Finland, moved to Sweden in 1944 and then to Canada in 1951. His collections of published verse include *Koputused Eneses (Inward Beats), Mârgid Mõtteliival (Marks On the Sands of Thought),* and *Tunnete Purdel (On the Footbridge of Feelings).* His essays and reviews have been published in various Estonian cultural magazines and newspapers.

From 1961 till 1965 LUIGI ROMEO was a Canadian immigrant and taught at the University of Toronto. Presently he is Chairman and Professor of Linguistics, Department of Linguistics, University of Colorado. Two of his books of poetry, *Battesimo* and *Triade Americana* have been published and his poems and articles have appeared in many scholarly and literary journals in several languages.

ANDREAS SCHROEDER is co-editor of *Contemporary Literature in Translation* and editor of *The League of Canadian Poets Newsletter.* He writes a regular column for *The Vancouver Province* and is a freelance broadcaster. His collections of poetry are *The Ozone Minotaur* (Sono Nis) and *File of Uncertainties. The Late Man,* his first collection of fiction, is to be released in the fall of 1971. He is the recipient of several Canada Council grants and has recently been awarded a grant by the Canadian Film Development Corporation to make a film of his story, *The Late Man.*

WACLAW IWANIUK is a poet, translator and essayist. He began publishing poetry while a student at the Free University in Warsaw. In 1938 he published his first book, *Fullness of June,* a long poem, *Day of Apocalyse,* and received his M.A. At the beginning of the Second World War, he joined the Polish Army in France and saw action in various spots in Europe. In 1946 he went to England where he studied at Cambridge University. In 1948 he came to Canada where he has since been employed at Toronto City Hall and by the Ontario Provincial government. In 1963 he received the Sulkowski Award. In 1964 his *Collected Poems* was published and The Literary Institute of Paris awarded him the Best Author's Prize for his literary achievements. In 1970 he won the Alfred Jurzykowski Foundation Award.

GUSTAW LINKE has translated much of Waclaw Iwaniuk's work. He lives in Toronto.

ZBIGNIEW FOLEJEWSKI is a professor of Slavonic Studies and Chairman of the

Comparative Literature program at the University of British Columbia. His scholarly articles have appeared in most of the distinguished journals of the world. Not the least of Professor Folejewski's garlands is that he was Czeslaw Milosz' first publisher, when they were at university together in Poland.

EINAR PALL JONSSON was born at Hareksstathir in Jökuldalur in eastern Iceland. He has been editor-in-chief of the weekly newspaper, *Logberg*, since 1927 (almost continuously). His work has been translated by many noted poets including Bliss Carman.

PAVEL JAVOR is the pen-name for George Skvor, born in Czechoslovakia. He took his Doctor of Law degree at Charles University in Prague, then his M.A. and Ph.D. from the University of Montreal. He has published twelve books of poems, three novels and many critical articles and studes. Since 1962 he has been *professeur à temps partiel* at the University of Montreal.

ALFRED FRENCH has translated much of Pavel Javor's work from Czech to French.

PROFESSOR WATSON KIRKCONNELL has translated much of the poetry written in Canada in languages other than English or French, into English. His languages include Czech, Icelandic, Ukranian, and German. He teaches at Acadia University.

BENNIE THOMSON, with Louis Dudek, translated *All of You* by Pavel Javor (Montreal, Delta, 1961).

REINHARD (Reinhard Walz) is presently a student at the University of British Columbia. Previously he studied at the University of Saskatchewan. He writes in both German and English. His work has appeared in *Contemporary Literature in Translation*, *The Canadian Fiction Magazine*, and *Prism international*. He is presently preparing, in English, a collection of lyric fiction for publication.

ANDRZEJ BUSZA's first book of poems in English translation, *Astrologer in the Underground*, has recently been published by the Ohio University Press. He is the author of a monograph on Conrad and a member of the London-based *Kontynenty* group of poets. He teaches in the English department at the University of British Columbia.

JAGNA BORAKS is a poet as well as a translator. Her poems and translations have been published in numerous journals including *Expression* (U.K.), *Oasis* (U.K.), and *Mundus Artium*.

ASTRID IVASK has published two collections of verse and essays in Latvian and translates from more than half a dozen languages. She now lives in Norman, Oklahoma where her husband is Professor of Comparative Literature and editor of the international literary quarterly, *Books Abroad*.

ARVED VIIRLAID was born in Estonia and educated at Kloostri and at the Tallinn State College of Fine Arts. After serving as an officer in the Finnish Army, he moved to Sweden in 1945, to England in 1946, and then to Canada in 1954. He first began publishing in 1939; since the war he's published four volumes of verse and six novels. His work has appeared in Latvian, Swedish, French, English, Spanish, Finnish, Ukranian, and Chinese, as well as his native Estonian.

TAIMI ENE MOKS was born on the island of Saaremaa in Estonia in 1935. She and her family emigrated to the United States in 1950. She is a graduate of the Latin American Institute in New York where she studied Spanish and techniques of translation. Presently she is a junior in Anthropology at the University of Washington. This is her first publication.

RAMON MANSOOR was born in Trinidad in 1944. In 1964 he came to Canada, completed his M.A. in Spanish Literature at Carleton University, and, at present he is completing his doctorate in Spanish Literature at Laval. He has taught at both Carleton and the University of Ottawa. His work has appeared in various Spanish language periodicals, his book, *Lirio Enamorado* was published by Industrias Graficas (Castile) in 1969.

YAR SLAVUTYCH is one of the most prolific Ukranian authors on the North American continent, and he stands in the vanguard of Ukranian poetry abroad. He was born in 1918 in the Ukraine where, in 1940, he graduated from the Pedagogic Institute in Azporizzja. He obtained his A.M. degree (1954) and Ph.D. (1955) from the University of Pennsylvania. Before coming to the University of Alberta in 1960, he served on the faculty of the United States Army Language School at Monterey, California. His publications ininclude *Spivale Kolos* (*The Singing Ears of Wheat*, Augsburg, 1945), *Homin Vikiv* (*The Echo of Ages*, Augsburg, 1946), *Pravdonosci* (*The Crusaders for Truth*, Munich, 1948), *Spraha* (*Thirst*, Frankfurt, 1950), *Don'ka bez imeny* (*The Daughter Without Name*, Buenos Aires, 1952), *Oaza* (*Oasis*, Edmonton, 1960), *Majestat* (*Majesty*, Edmonton, 1962), *Trofeji* (*Trophies*, Edmonton, 1963), and *Zavojovnyky prerij* (*The Conquerors of Prairies*, Edmonton, 1968). He has also published numerous literary articles and book reviews in both Ukranian and English. Yar Slavutych is an author of *Conversational Ukranian, I* and *II* (Winnipeg, Edmonton, 1959, 1960). His poems have been translated into German, Russian, Spanish, Byelorussian, and English. The English edition, *Oasis* (New York, 1959), represents, in the author's opinion, the best the author has written during the previous two decades of his creativity.

MYRA HAAS has also translated the work of Yar Slavutych for broadcast by the C.B.C.

Like T. Hiramatus, TAKEO NAKANO is a Toronto poet.